THE BIBLICAL JOURNEY
OF FAITH

THE BIBLICAL JOURNEY OF FAITH

Frank R. VanDevelder

FORTRESS PRESS
PHILADELPHIA

Passages in which the RSV has been altered for the sake of inclusive language.

Page	Verses	Page	Verses
15	Gen. 2:18	101	Mark 1:17
15–16	Gen. 12:2–3	101	John 15:13–14
38	Exod. 3:14	102	Matt. 16:24
49	Deut. 8:3	102	Mark 4:23
72	Ps. 39:4–6, 11	102	Luke 8:21
84	Acts 17:24	105	Col. 3:11
96	John 20:17	105	Gal. 3:6–9
98	Matt. 25:37–40		

Library of Congress Cataloging-in-Publication Data

VanDevelder, Frank R.
The biblical journey of faith.

Bibliography: p.
1. Emigration and immigration in the Bible.
2. Emigration and immigration—Religious aspects—
Christianity.   3. Christian life—1960-   . I. Title.
BS680.E38V36   1988   220.8'3048   88-45250
ISBN 0-8006-2318-5

Printed in the United States of America   1-2318

94   93   91   90   2   3   4   5   6   7   8   9   10

In Memoriam
Robert O. Kevin
1899–1987

CONTENTS

PREFACE

IN THIS BOOK I am inviting you to take a journey with me. The mode of travel is by foot, so the route we follow can be called a road or path, and the journey itself is a walk. The journey of which I speak is one of encounter with the Bible, and with God through the Bible. The road that we follow will lead us through the Bible, as Christians define it, from beginning to end.

The itinerary of this tour, its selectivity and pace, assumes some prior knowledge of the Bible on the part of the traveler. It is not a trip for the novice or for the expert guide. It falls somewhere in between. It is for the traveler who has some acquaintance with biblical terrain and would like more.

The notes are designed with this audience in mind. Most of them are meant for the traveler who wants to go a little beyond the limits of this particular journey, perhaps to strike out on an interesting sidetrip.

The promise I hold out is not only that this trip will be enjoyable and informative but also that through walking this road, you will come to a deeper understanding of God, yourself, and the territory of human life and history. I can make such a promise with confidence because the main subject of interest on our journey is not the book you have in your hands, but the Bible. This book is a guide to the Bible itself, so do not neglect to read the portions of the Bible referred to in the text.

Work on this book began during a sabbatical leave from the Protestant Episcopal Theological Seminary in Virginia in 1976–77, when I was a resident Fellow at the Ecumenical Institute for Theological

THE BIBLICAL JOURNEY OF FAITH

Studies at Tantur, between Jerusalem and Bethlehem. I am grateful to Virginia Seminary for that leave, to the Evangelical Education Society of the Episcopal Church for a grant which made it possible to spend the year in Jerusalem, and to the Ecumenical Institute at Tantur for providing such an ideal environment for study and growth.

The manuscript lay unfinished for several years. From Dr. John A. Hollar of Fortress Press I received both encouragement to complete it and the expert editorial guidance needed to improve its style, clarity, and focus. I am grateful to him.

Work on the subject-matter of this project goes back to my doctoral dissertation on the Abrahamic covenant traditions written at Drew University under the guidance of professors Larry Toombs, Bernhard Anderson, and James F. Ross. In fact, it really goes back further, to my first studies of biblical theology and of Abraham under professors Robert Kevin (deceased), Murray Newman, Richard Reid, A. T. Mollegen (deceased), and Holt Graham at the Virginia Theological Seminary. To all of these guides along the way go my sincere thanks.

But finally, my deepest gratitude belongs to my wife Mary, my companion-sojourner and a never-failing source of strength and joy on the journey that we have made together.

PROLOGUE

LARGE NUMBERS of people in the world today know something of the life of the sojourner. Millions are on the move. Hundreds of thousands are forced to flee earthquakes, volcanoes, flood, or famine; others flee cruel and powerful oppressors or the worst disaster of all—war. Even in areas relatively free from such catastrophes, large numbers of people stay in one place for only a few years at a time. I notice that many have the same problem I do in answering the questions "Where's your home?" or "Where are you from?" To the first, I usually reply, "Home is where my hat is." To the second, I equivocate: "Do you mean, 'Where was I born?' or 'Where did I last live?'"

Most of us are surprised when we meet one of those rare individuals who has lived in the same place for an entire lifetime. Clearly, the inhabitants of this planet are on the move. Even those who manage to "stay put" are not immune to this sense of mobility and the disorientation that it produces. The world itself is changing so rapidly that people experience psychological displacement even while staying in the same spot. "Future shock" makes sojourners of us all.

This widespread mobility creates problems. Although some people relish it, a great many do not like this mobile way of life. This is sometimes expressed only as a vague uneasiness about the way things are; at other times, it is a well articulated discontent. Many families turn their backs on a promotion and higher income rather than have to move again.

There has been much discussion of rootlessness as a factor in emotional problems, or as a contributing cause of some kinds of disturbed behavior in both juveniles and adults. Books and plays about "roots" have enjoyed success in recent years. It seems that most of us are not overjoyed about our sojourner-like existence.

I believe that the Bible has something very important to say to people, whether Jews or Christians, with such a problem. Those whose faith is guided and nourished by the Bible will see that the problem posed by our sojourner-like existence is dealt with in the Bible—at length and in depth.

I write as a Christian from a Christian perspective. But the issue that we are discussing is dealt with in both the Hebrew Bible, traditionally called the Old Testament by Christians, and the Christian Scriptures, traditionally called the New Testament. The problem is a common one of human existence, and both bodies of Scripture approach it from a similar perspective. This commonality is underlined by my use of "people of God" to refer to all those Jews or Christians who live out of the rich treasury of biblical revelation. I also use the designations B.C.E. (Before the Common Era) and C.E. (Common Era) to indicate the shared history of Jews and Christians across the centuries. These are more inclusive and universal designations than B.C. and A.D.

Inclusiveness also has to do with gender. The opening chapters of this study deal with the patriarchal age, in which it was assumed that a woman was related to the deity primarily through her father or her husband or the chief of the clan. It is clear that women took part in decisions regarding family moves (Gen. 31:14–16), and that the faith of the patriarchs was shared by the matriarchs (Gen. 17:15–16). Nevertheless, the language of the biblical text focuses almost exclusively on the relationship between God and the male head of the clan, who represented all other members of his household. We read the story recognizing that the language is culturally conditioned and does not adequately represent the reality of the situation, but we cannot totally modernize the language without introducing anachronism.

Some words are also necessary about the term "sojourner," since it is not a household term today. It originated in Old French, according to the Oxford English Dictionary, but seems to have come into English speech through its use in the King James Version of the Bible as the translation of the Hebrew word *ger* with which we shall be dealing. The word "sojourner" was retained in the Revised Standard

Version (RSV), as shown in many of the key texts that we shall be examining. Presumably the RSV translators either felt no need or were unable to improve upon it.

Nevertheless, "sojourner" sounds archaic to people whose ears have not become accustomed to those particular English translations of the Bible. I have tried several alternatives. "Resident alien" is perhaps the most accurate translation for the word *ger* in the Hebrew Bible, but it is cumbersome and has a distinctly legal flavor. In fact, every alternative that I have considered had to be rejected because it led the mind in the wrong direction, or had connotations that were unfortunate or misleading for our subject. "Sojourner" conveys the idea, but at the same time is neutral enough to allow for the colorations that gather around the concept without locking the mind exclusively onto one or another of them. I have kept it, therefore, as the best overall designation for the subject at hand.

We must necessarily deal with words, but this is not a "word study." "Sojourner" is a word symbol, a pictorial image, drawn from the biblical story which depicts our life before God and with God.

— 1 —

ABRAHAM
THE
SOJOURNER

THE FIRST ELEVEN chapters of Genesis paint, with broad strokes and somber tones, a picture of the predicament of the human race upon God's good earth. Within the universe which God created and approved as "very good," human beings, who share in that approval, embark upon a course which leads to fratricide (Genesis 4) and then to a total breakdown in communication, with the resulting dispersal of the human family across the face of the earth (Genesis 11). It is a dark and tragic story of accelerating degeneration, which repeatedly requires intervention by the Creator in order to prevent the premature collapse of the whole enterprise. Human life has become the opposite of what God intended it to be.

This is the somber setting for the dramatic story of God's intervention to do something to save the human race from its tragic predicament.[1] That story begins with a word, a message from God to one individual.

> Now the LORD said to Abram, "Go from your country and your kindred and your father's house to the land that I will show you." (Gen. 12:1)

It is clear from the outset that Abram (later Abraham; and Sarai becomes Sarah, Genesis 17) is being called to a completely new life based on different principles from those which undergird the lives of his relatives and neighbors.[2] It is not just that he is taking part in a migratory movement. Thousands of people had migrated before Abraham did, for all kinds of reasons. Abraham is being called to a new way of life based upon a reality different from that which

15

undergirds the lives of his contemporaries. This call involves separation. Abraham is being *called out* from the certainties and assurances
on which his neighbors' lives are built. He is being asked to abandon
that way of life and its foundations, that whole civilization—the
accumulation, through centuries, of a system of thought and action,
of mythologies, economic organization, technology, and social
structures—all the things which people in their normal round of
daily living take for granted. He is called to abandon the assumptions
on which life there was based, on which his own life and the life of
his family had thus far been based.

The radical nature of the break which is called for and the ex-
treme difficulty of it for Abraham are poignantly stressed in the
threefold phrase of Gen. 12:1, which may be thought of as three
concentric circles with Abraham at the center. The command
moves from the most distant social unit ("country") to the clan
("kindred") to the most intimate family circle ("father's house"), and
with each step the emotional difficulty of the departure increases.
Abraham is called to leave behind all of the securities that normally
surround and support life, and simply "Go out!"

On what basis? With what in view? What is there in the call that
would justify the risk? What assurance is he given? What will take
the place of those foundations for life which he is being asked to
abandon?

And where can he find the strength to take such a step? The
answer is simple: in the message which he has received. That message
comes to him from a Speaker who addresses him personally. Like all
words of personal address, this one carries with it something of the
Speaker himself. Abraham is confronted and addressed as a person.
The first thing to which he is being called by this word is a relationship, a personal relationship of trust. This word, which comes crash-
ing into Abraham's consciousness from somewhere outside the
world he has known until this moment, is addressed to him personally. It establishes his personal identity and opens up before him the
possibility for a life-changing relationship.

This word addressed to Abraham is more than a personal greeting.
It is a word of promise and a word of command. It is a call to trust and
commitment, to obedience, responsibility, and hope.

16

The first part of the message is the command. It is breathtaking in what it takes for granted! "Leave behind everything you have ever trusted in before, and trust in me alone—in me and my word to you." What a dignity is conferred on the recipient in the mere fact that he is honored with such a command! This command tells us much about Abraham as God saw him.

No guarantees are given to make things easier. The destination of the journey is not even named. Everything, absolutely everything, rests in the One who calls! When family and friends ask Abraham and Sarah where they are headed on this foolhardy journey, they cannot even tell them. "To a land that I will show you" is all they have been told. They must rest their faith entirely in the One who is calling them.

The message, however, is not merely a command. In fact, the element of command does not really come first. The fact that God has chosen Abraham and Sarah as the ones who would receive this word precedes the command. They are invited to enter a relationship. The word contains not only requirement but also promise. The promise precedes the command implicitly and follows it explicitly. The two elements—promise and command—are interwoven.

Every relationship between persons has this dual aspect. It has, on the one hand, a certain shape, certain limits. The relationship exists within a set of requirements that constitute the definition of the relationship. At the same time, every personal relationship has a promise intrinsic within it. It promises life, fulfillment, enrichment, meaningful destiny. Truly human life is not possible without personal relationships. "It is not good for human beings to be alone" (Gen. 2:18).

It is the promise which provides the mainspring, the motivation, the power for the relationship. We cannot know in advance what a relationship will produce. The enormous possibilities which lie hidden in the relationship urge us onward and enable us to accept the invitation with its intrinsic demand and risk.

The command to Abraham has scarcely been pronounced when the dimensions of the promise are spelled out. What a rich and many-sided promise it is!

> And I will make of you a great nation, and I will bless you, and make your name great, so that you will be a blessing. I will bless those who

bless you, and the one who curses you I will curse; and by you all the
families of the earth shall bless themselves [or, in you all the families of
the earth shall be blessed]. (Gen. 12:2-3)

The fulfillment of this promise rests entirely with the One who is
speaking. The promise is not self-fulfilling. In other words, the
promise is a promise only within the realm of the relationship. It does
not exist outside it. Everything, therefore, depends on the nature of
the One who calls and promises. Is the Promiser able and willing to
fulfill the promise? Can the one called depend on that?

From the standpoint of the one called, there is no way to eliminate
the risk involved in accepting the call. The invitation is to a relationship of trust. There is nothing to go on but the bare word. The leap
of faith is essential if there is to be a positive response at all.

"So Abram went, as the LORD had told him" (Gen. 12:4a). His
response is one of both faith and obedience. The two are inseparable;
their unity is shown clearly here. Faith, in the biblical understanding,
is trust and commitment, and these involve the whole person. Therefore, faith issues in deeds. In biblical usage faith can never be a matter
of the mind alone; it involves the person as a totality. Thus the
invitation is accepted by one's acting upon it. For Abraham, to trust is
to pack up and depart! The action shows the trust. Faith and obedience may be separated in theoretical discussion, but never in life.

The basic nature of Abraham's call and the life of faith to which he
is called never change throughout his lifetime. The relationship to
which he is called, which is later defined as a covenant, continues to
be one of trust and obedience for Abraham. Everything depends on
this relationship. It is the most important thing in his life. This is the
foundation that replaces all other foundations, the base from which
life is henceforth to be lived, the reality which determines everything
in Abraham's future.

Thus Abraham, in accepting the call, becomes the prototype of all
those who find their foundation for life and their security in a relationship like this one, and in nothing else.

ABRAHAM AS FOUNDING ANCESTOR

In order to assess the significance of this story for Abraham's
descendants, then and now, we must carefully notice his position in
the biblical story and what that means.

Abraham's journey to Canaan with Sarah and the rest of the clan, their moving around in the land, journey to Egypt, return to Mamre, and all of their subsequent experiences now stand at the beginning of a collection of patriarchal stories in Genesis 12—50. Abraham's position at the head of the list of patriarchs has great importance for the history of these traditions and their influence on the lives of those who follow. That importance does not lie in the significance of Abraham as an individual, or even as the head of a clan, so much as in Abraham's status as "founding father," the corporate embodiment and prototype of the life of the whole people who look back to him as their ancestor.

In order to realize why this is so, two factors in ancient Near Eastern ways of thinking must be taken into account.

1. Much importance is attached to beginnings. People of that time and place felt that in order to understand an entity, one needed to learn the story of its origin, because the whole of its life history was already present, encapsulated in seed form as it were, in that beginning. This was true of a family, a nation, an institution, a world.[3] What the thing would become is already there in that originating, primal moment. Today we are thinking in a somewhat parallel way about the growth of biological organisms from a single cell which contains the "code" (DNA) to the nature of the organism that will grow from it. For the ancient, this kind of thinking is applied to a wider range of phenomena, including human society and the whole cosmos; it embraces history as well as biology. This can be expressed quite realistically when it is said that the descendants of the ancestor of a certain people are "in his loins" already (Gen. 35:11 KJV, King James Version). But more important, the destiny of those descendants is already prefigured in the story of his life. His story is their story in condensed narrative form.

2. These ancients also held the concept of "corporate personality." In place of our sharp distinction between the individual and the group, the ancient Israelite had a more dynamic and fluid way of perceiving that relation. A group could see itself as embodied in a certain individual. That individual is no longer just an individual, but takes on a corporate identity. The individual is the group. This could be true of a living leader, especially the king. The fate of the whole people rides with the king in battle. When King Ahab falls dead in

his chariot, "a cry went through the army, 'Every man to his city and every man to his country!'" (1 Kings 22:36). The troops disperse in panic. They have fallen with their leader.

This must be understood more realistically than is our conception of the psychological influence of a leader. Perhaps a pale residue of this idea remains today in the symbolic significance which nations often attach to leaders, especially in a real or quasi monarchy. Charles DeGaulle could say, "I am France." The British monarch certainly had this significance at one time, although it is greatly weakened today. For ancient people, it was true in a more realistic and powerful way.

This concept of corporate personality can also be applied to someone in the past, especially, in a patriarchal society, the originating male ancestor. The whole clan or tribe sees itself as united psychically in the originating patriarch. Once again, this seems to be more thoroughgoing and realistic than anything we Americans might mean when we speak of George Washington as our founding father. Even the legends about Abraham Lincoln, which have stamped themselves on our corporate consciousness to a greater degree than those about George Washington, do not approach the way in which the ancient tribes and their founding patriarch were merged into a kind of psychic unity as reflected in stories which get told and retold, generation after generation.

This way of thinking about the relation between "the one and the many" together with the importance attached to beginnings help to explain the significance of the Hebrew patriarchs for the tribes that regard themselves as descendants of the patriarchs, especially of the one who heads the list. The question as to which patriarch stands *first* in the tribal memories of a people who sees itself as having descended from several such patriarchs is not just a matter of casual historical interest. The one who heads the list becomes the embodiment of the life of this people, whose destiny is spelled out in the stories about the patriarch which are preserved and handed down.

Thus Abraham is the "one" in whose life story the history of the "many" is prefigured. Abraham's position at the beginning of the story invests all that takes place in his life with extraordinary significance that goes far beyond historical interest as we would normally define it. People in Jerusalem at least from the time of Solomon (tenth century B.C.E.) and probably earlier would have read or heard the story of Abraham with overtones such as these.[4]

If Abraham is viewed as an archetypal symbol for the whole life of Israel, it follows that the people of Israel would have had a strong interest in his character and his life. What could Israel expect, if its destiny was prefigured in his story? And we, too, would like to know what we can learn about ourselves, if we are, in some sense, his descendants. In outline, we can say the following things about Abraham on the basis of the Genesis stories:

1. Abraham is called. He hears God's voice.
2. He responds in faith to that call, and embarks on a journey to an unknown destination.
3. After that destination has been revealed and reached, Abraham sojourns in that land in the light of his call and the promise that it contained.

From beginning to end, Abraham lives by the word that he received from the God who called him.

That does not mean that Abraham is never tempted to abandon the road of trust. On the contrary, he is repeatedly tempted to look for security somewhere else. The road of faith is never smooth or easy. Abraham is constantly confronted with the temptation, now subtle, now blatant, to find some other way. He is tempted to make the new world like the old one, to find ways to fulfill the word of promise himself, to find even a temporary resting place for his faith, other than in the One. But even in his temptation, faltering, and failure of faith, Abraham is still the prototype. His descendants can still see themselves in him, straying from the path, faltering, objecting.

See how Abraham tries to find some other way (Genesis 16)! The strain of following the word of promise becomes too great. Years pass and the promised offspring, on whom everything else in the promise seems to depend, does not arrive. Abraham and Sarah grow older. The options for the fulfilling of the promise grow fewer in their minds, and they see the time ahead when all possibility for fulfillment will be closed out. Some action must be taken! Perhaps the One who had given them the promise had intended Abraham and Sarah to take some initiative in working out this matter. If Sarah is barren, there is a customary process by which offspring can be gotten through Sarah's maid and legally belong to Abraham.[5] The plan is carried through, a son is born, and soon the festival of weaning is celebrated.

Only at that moment, when Abraham is resting in the assurance that his plan has worked, does the One who called at the first suddenly speak again: "That child is not the child of promise, Abraham." The promise must remain a promise. It cannot be brought under the control of the recipient. Abraham's role is to accept the promise, cling to it, live toward it, but not to fulfill it. His only correct response is trust that the One who called will carry out that word.

Birth to Prayer The promise creates a future. The only road to that future is trust. This other road which Abraham has tried is a dead-end street. It leads nowhere. It stops all forward movement, because it is not the road of trust. It was embarked upon because faith had faltered. Some other basis for life had been sought—human reason, practicality, cleverness, logic, resourcefulness—in short, the resources of Abraham himself.

Abraham was not called out of Mesopotamia to follow such a road as this. It cannot succeed! He is allowed no resting place for faith, no foundation for life, save One.

The word that is sometimes used to describe Abraham after he has reached the land of Canaan and pitched his tent there is the Hebrew word *ger*, usually translated "sojourner" (Gen. 23:4). It is a good word to sum up what Abraham typifies for the people of God. A sojourner in a society stands somewhere between the native-born person and the complete foreigner, a resident alien who has no permanent possession or natural rights in the place in which she or he dwells.

Abraham comes into the land of Canaan, the land to which he has been led by the promise, as a sojourner. The land is not his. He pitches his tent in it (Gen. 13:18) and enjoys the goodness of its fruits, but he does not possess it. It is called "the land of his sojournings" (Gen. 17:8; Exod. 6:4).[6] The land itself is not the foundation for his life. His hopes are not built upon it. He is a sojourner in it. He lives in the land by faith, in hope.

His presence in the land is due to the One who called him out of a very different place to this place. That call was not just a relocation. He was called out of that "world," that whole way of existence, to a new one. Abraham's life was not simply transplanted, it was transformed. He was not led to Canaan simply in order to live there as he had lived in Ur of the Chaldeans. It is not just the place that is new; all things have become new because of that call and the relationship which it initiated. Inevitably, then, Abraham's relation to this land is different from his relation to his old land. Back in Mesopotamia, the land itself was one of the foundations for life, along with air and water, sky and planets, sun and moon.[7] Abraham has been called out of that world to a way of living in which the One who called is the only foundation for life, one whose word is the only life-giving source of strength.

Hence the land to which Abraham is led is a land of promise. Just as abundant offspring are received first in the form of promise, so the land is received as promise. One can only live in a land of promise as a *ger*, a sojourner. Abraham cannot establish, invent, discover, or create any foundations on which to rest his faith other than the word of the One.

The promise of the land is a genuine promise that will be fulfilled. There is no doubt about that. Abraham's descendants will possess the land, just as surely as Abraham now possesses the child. The question is not whether the promise will be fulfilled, but how to live by faith in the Promiser before and after the fulfillment.

The offspring is a promised blessing; the land is a promised blessing. Abraham is not even permitted to place his faith in the blessing itself, but only in the Giver. This is made clear in the story of the journey to the mount of sacrifice with young Isaac (Genesis 22).[8] The question posed there is: Where does Abraham's faith rest now—in the promised offspring at his side, or in the Promiser? Abraham superbly meets the test. He does not cling to the gift. In effect, he returns it to the Giver. To the Giver alone he clings!

The principle illustrated so powerfully in that story with respect to the promised child is equally true of the promise of the land. No more than in the case of his son is Abraham allowed to rest his faith in the land of Canaan. In the case of the land, this is expressed, not in a story, but simply in the word *ger*: Abraham is "a sojourner in the land." Of course there is now a difference between the two promises: that of the child has been fulfilled; that of the land awaits future fulfillment. The promise of the land is for the time of Abraham's descendants. They will be tested about that promise.

Abraham never ceases being a sojourner in the land. He is called to live on the basis of the promise all the way to the end. He faces the future and lives toward it with hope. Only at the moment of death does he cease being a sojourner in the land (Genesis 23). He asks the Hittites among whom he sojourns to sell him one piece of land with a cave in it as a burial place for Sarah and himself (Gen. 23:4). Thus, from the time of the call to the hour of their death, Abraham and Sarah are sojourners in the land of promise.[9]

This is the picture we are given: one called by God responds in faith, enters a relationship of trust and obedience, and lives out his life on the basis of the promise as a sojourner in the land. The word "sojourner" is only a point of entry into the story. It is the story that tells the tale, and that story cannot be compressed into one word.

The character of Abraham is a model for the biblical people of God. The elements of this story—call, faithful response, life in cov-enant with and in total reliance upon God—describe the kind of life that Abraham's descendants are called to live.

—2—

FAITH
FOR PEOPLE
ON THE MOVE

THE FIRST OF Abraham's many descendants, as Genesis introduces them to us, are the other patriarchs and matriarchs, the clan-ancestors whose cultural context and way of life, while so far removed from our own, are quite similar to those of Abraham. We will focus on the final form of their stories as given to us by the Bible, and introduce the results of historical research when they add depth to our understanding of the subject.

Of those who claim physical descent from Abraham, Genesis traces in detail only the family history of those who follow in the line of the promise, for this is a story about God's word of promise and command. It is the unfolding of the promise which leads the story forward toward the accomplishment of God's purpose.

The stories which follow Genesis 23 are so filled with the details of family life that the kind of relationship which we observed between God and Abraham seems to get lost or obscured in the round of mundane occurrences described. We find ourselves wondering: Is there a genuine continuity between the faith of Abraham and Sarah described in Genesis 12—22, and the lives of Isaac and Rebekah, Jacob, Leah and Rachel, and their clans which follow?

In the middle half of the Book of Genesis (chaps. 12—35), the relationship between God and Abraham, which is now spoken of as a covenant (Genesis 15 and 17), is renewed for Isaac and then for Jacob. This means that the call originally directed to Abraham has been extended to his descendants. Since their circumstances are quite different from those of Abraham when he first received that call in

Mesopotamia, the call takes a different form for them, but the basic ingredients are the same. They too are invited into a relationship that requires trust and obedience; for them too that invitation contains elements of both promise and requirement. Isaac is commanded to remain in the land, and is promised God's presence and the fulfill-ment of all that had been promised to Abraham (Gen. 26:1-4, 23-24). For Jacob, the command varies from time to time, and the promises are expanded (Gen. 28:13-15; 31:3; 35:1-4, 9-15).

It is apparent to the reader of the Bible that the religion of the patriarchal age is quite different in many respects from the religion of the periods that follow. The forms and institutions of worship differ from those of the period of Moses, just as much as those of Moses' age differ from those of the monarchy of Solomon's time. In the Genesis stories there are no buildings set aside for worship. Holy places are in the open, and often associated with a certain tree, stone, brook, river, or well. The crucial item is the stone altar, presumably to be used for animal sacrifice. There is no priestly hierarchy and no mention of vestments, utensils, or priestly apparatus as we find later. The father of the clan is the priest. Religion, like all of life, centers in the family and the clan. Such is the general picture that Genesis gives us of patriarchal religion.[1]

LITERARY TRANSMISSION OF THE PATRIARCHAL STORIES

One needs to be aware that the stories about the patriarchal families were handed down through many centuries of both oral and written transmission.[2] One would expect them to undergo a certain amount of reshaping and updating as they passed from generation to generation, and as the frames of reference (literary, social, cultural, religious) within which they were spoken and heard changed from one age to another. This is what actually happened! These stories continued to be living traditions which spoke anew to each genera-tion. The people of God pass on the traditions in which they still hear God speaking to them, and in which they still find, in their own day, a basis for self-understanding and power for daily living.

The Genesis picture of patriarchal religion, therefore, has been somewhat modified via that process of transmission and reinterpreta-tion through the centuries. But it also seems evident that the religious practices and institutions of a later age (e.g., the monarchy) have not, to any significant degree, been "read back" into the time of the patriarchs in these narratives. The picture we are given of patriarchal religion is either an authentic one, coming out of patriarchal life itself, or else it is a literary construction with deliberate archaizing intentions.

A few decades ago many scholars believed that almost nothing could be said historically about the era of the patriarchs because all of the material in Genesis was written in a much later age. It was therefore thought to be a literary retrojection of ideas and materials that really originated in the time of the Israelite monarchy or later.[3] Today, such a view is probably no longer that of the majority. In part, this change is the result of new methods of literary investigation. To an even greater extent, it is the result of archaeological discoveries and the refinement of the methodology for interpreting the data from those discoveries.[4]

Although the dating of the patriarchal traditions and of the patriarchs themselves is still being debated,[5] we can now affirm that the stories, at many points, are compatible with what has been learned about life in the Fertile Crescent in the second millennium B.C.E. It thus seems likely that the core of these stories originated in the premonarchical period, even though they were later modified, reshaped, or reinterpreted through continued use in the life of the Israelite community. In particular, the picture of the patriarchs' religion in Genesis fits well with what has been learned about the religions of the world in the patriarchs' time.

An analogy may be useful for describing what has happened to our understanding of the Bible in the past century. You may have had the experience of attending a play when, at a certain point, everything in the theater was plunged into total darkness for some seconds. Then a single circle of light appeared on the stage with one or two actors in the circle. As they spoke to one another, all eyes concentrated on that circle of light, and nothing existed outside of it. Suddenly, all the stage lights were turned on, and the two people in the spotlight blended into a larger scene with dozens of people moving about. The others had been there all along, invisible in the darkness. The scene in the spotlight, which before had existed in total isolation and independence, became part of a larger tableau.

Not too many years ago, the personalities of the Hebrew Bible were somewhat like those figures in the spotlight. We knew that there were other peoples around, because the Bible told us so, but we knew very little about them. In effect, the biblical characters seemed to be moving independently, in a circle of divine light, quite isolated from the surrounding world. Hence everything about them was assumed to be unique. But now the lights have gone on all around, and we see that the stage for their drama is peopled by a large stream of humanity, coming and going across that little part of the world called Canaan on the eastern shore of the Mediterranean Sea.[6] We now see the people of the Bible as part of a world with which they shared words, tools, ideas, and institutions. Even the structural elements and cultic details of their religion, for the most part, are seen to belong within the general context of the religions of their world.

If this results in the loss of some of our sense of the uniqueness of the biblical people and their history, there is a compensating gain in the historical realism with which we are now able to look at them. We are now better prepared to see them as real people living in a real historical setting with all of its complexities, ambiguities, and problems. If we have to work harder to discover what is different about their faith, the recompense is that the result of our search will be more relevant and applicable to our own lives. It is sometimes said that when historical research does its job well, the distance between the modern world and the biblical world becomes ever wider. We see more clearly how far removed from them we are in time and space, in customs and world view. But there is a deeper sense in which the opposite is true. Historical research also narrows the gap! The better we can see them as real people struggling with the forces and issues of a real historical existence which is not essentially different from our own, the more their message of faith has to say to us and the better we are able to hear it.

CHARACTERISTIC FEATURES OF
PATRIARCHAL RELIGION

We now want to focus on the characteristic features and central elements in the faith of the patriarchs. If we can isolate these, then we should be able to see more clearly how patriarchal religion compares with the other religions of its environment, and also how it is related to the religion of Moses' time which immediately follows in the biblical story.

Among the primary characteristics of patriarchal religion are the four that follow.

1. *Interest is centered in a personal relationship between the patriarch and God.* At the center of this faith stands a theophany, an unusual event of such importance for the patriarch and his family that their lives are never the same again.[7] At a certain moment, the patriarch is surprised by a voice speaking to him from the divine realm (Gen. 12:1; 26:2, 3; 28:13; 35:11ff.). In a world in which many gods are assumed to exist, one deity has chosen to appear to this person, to initiate a relationship with him, and to take him and his family under special protection.

The one thus honored is blessed by this encounter with the deity, and the blessing is "contagious." It flows to the people around him.[8] It even "rubs off" on people whose lives touch his only tangentially (Gen. 26:28–29; 12:3). Since the patriarch is regarded as the center of life and the representative of the whole clan in this society, the personal encounter between him and his god affects the life of everyone in the clan. All members come within the orbit of the blessing and the promise given by the deity. And since it is through their father that they are related to this deity, they often speak of the god who appeared to him as "the god of our father," even though that god has a proper name which they may know well.[9] There is some indication that the clans of the three major patriarchs and matriarchs in Genesis once spoke of the deity who had taken them under his special care as the "Benefactor of Abraham" (Gen. 15:1), the "Fear of Isaac" (Gen. 31:42, 53) and the "Bull [or "Mighty One"] of Jacob" (Gen. 49:24).[10] In one of these encounters, however, we are specifically told that the deity refused to reveal his name to the patriarch (Gen. 32:29). So the clan might speak of him in general terms as "the god of our father" (Gen. 25:24; 28:13).

The central element of this religion, therefore, is the personal relationship between the patriarch, representing his clan, and the deity who singled him out and appeared to him. But a word of caution is necessary here. "Personal" does not mean "private" or "individual" in the context of patriarchal society. The relationship of the deity is with the father, the mother, and the whole clan. Furthermore, it can be passed on to their descendants, since the blessing promised to the "father" in these encounters specifically includes the generations to come (Gen. 13:15–16; 22:17–18; 26:3–4).

2. *Closely related to the first feature is the element of freedom.* There is a voluntary quality about this relationship. The deity freely chooses to invite this particular person/clan into a relationship. Likewise the patriarch freely chooses to respond positively to the invitation. The fact that both parties enter the relationship voluntarily gives it a very different quality from some of the other divine-human encounters in the religions of that time. Since there is no compulsion or inescapable necessity about it, the relationship is morally binding in an inward sense which could not be true of a relationship about which the parties had no choice.

3. *Also related to the centrality of personal relationship is the priority of the word in this faith.* The relationship begins with a word addressed to the patriarch. Although the element of vision is not totally lacking, and even dreams can sometimes be the medium of communication, the norm is a personal and specific message addressed to the patriarch. That word sets this moment of revelation apart from experiences of wordless awe in the presence of the numinous which abound in other religions of that day (and this). The patriarch is sometimes silent in these stories, but God is not.

One result of this priority of the word is the fact that this is a religion without images. Nothing is said in any of these stories about making an image of the deity. Jacob's entourage, for instance, is instructed to put away their foreign gods (idols) before beginning a pilgrimage to Bethel to build an altar to the God who had appeared to Jacob there (Gen. 35:2–4). No description of the deity is given. Most of the reports of divine communication give only the words that were spoken. When there is a visionary element, as in Jacob's dream, it is of secondary importance and drops out of sight completely once God has begun to speak (Gen. 28:13–15). It is the word that is of central importance here.[11]

4. *Consistent with the priority of the word, which always contains both promise and command, patriarchal religion is concerned with time, primarily the future.* The relationship being established is the beginning of something which moves forward into the future with great hope.[12] Everything depends on the future unfolding of the

divine plan ("to a land that I will show you") and the fulfilling of the divine promise ("I will give you . . . I will make of you . . . you shall be . . . I will be with you. . . . I will keep you.").

This concern with time does not exclude interest in the dimension of space, of course. At times there is a genuine interest in places, especially when they are related to the promise (Gen. 12:7). But concern about space is mostly expressed in connection with the land as a whole. The two dimensions of time and space are combined in a phrase: "the Promised Land."

Again and again in the divine messages to the patriarchs, interest centers in the future. It is the period of time which stretches from the moment when the promise was first given to the moment of its eventual fulfillment which is of interest. This concentration on the future does not mean that there is no interest in the past, but even when such an interest is expressed, its primary focus is on the future. The past is very important indeed for plotting the path which the promise took as it moved forward toward the future. To Isaac, God says, "I will fulfill the oath which I swore to your father Abraham" (Gen. 26:3). As Jacob is addressed by God in the *present*, he is reminded of the *past* ("I am the LORD, the God of Abraham your father") and pointed to the *future* ("I will keep you . . . and will bring you back to this land," Gen. 28:13–15). The line drawn through these three points in time opens up the possibility of experiencing and conceptualizing a unified history, but only because the main thrust of the message is toward the future.[13]

The story of the patriarchs moves toward a historical goal. The driving force behind this movement is the promise. It is the will of God who spoke the word of promise which creates the future toward which the story moves. And move it does, in spite of all the obstacles which get in the way and have to be overcome.

These four features, in combination, chart a course for patriarchal religion which moves in a very different direction from the one taken by the other religions of the great river basins in Egypt and Mesopotamia and the religions of nearer neighbors like the Canaanites.

For example, the focus on personal relationship, combined with the emphasis on time rather than space, produces a religion which is at odds with the strong attachment to cultic objects and places that characterizes other religions of the ancient Near East. Patriarchal

31

religion is not "tied down" to a particular spot. It is well suited to the life of a mobile group of people. Even though the initial appearance of the deity to the clan-ancestor "takes place" at a particular location, that spot does not become determinative for this religion. The "God of the fathers" is not limited to one geographical area. God speaks with Abraham, for example, at Haran in Mesopotamia, at Shechem, at Bethel, at Mamre, on a mountain in the land of Moriah, and at several other unidentified places, and also intervenes on Abraham's behalf down in Egypt and at Gerar. Abraham does not have to return to the place at which he first met God in order to continue the relationship. God appears at a particular place (a necessity if the appearance is to take place at all!), but is not limited to that place.

It seems that Jacob did not fully understand this before his dream at Bethel (see Gen. 28:10–22). That may be the reason he was so surprised at what happened to him there. This story about Jacob illustrates the connection between patriarchal religion and holy places, as well as a number of other aspects of patriarchal faith. We want to know how God reveals himself to Jacob and how God reveals himself to us.

First, we see in this story that *God encounters us as we are on the road*, in the midst of the journey. God meets us as we go about the ordinary or extraordinary tasks of our lives: seeking a mate, looking for a new job, fleeing from danger, seeking escape from a difficult situation or relationship, searching for identity—all of these might describe what Jacob was doing when he was encountered by God. Jacob was on the move from his father's house in Beersheba to the ancestral home in Haran. He had left home, security, affection, and dependency behind. He had also left an angry brother, a dangerous threat, and an unhappy family situation. The revelation from God came in the middle of a personal history, as Jacob was on the road. In this fact we already see a major difference between this God and the other gods that people worshiped in Jacob's day. This God does not reveal himself primarily in the warm rays of the sun, the thunder and rainfall of the storm, or the fertility of field and flock and family, although he has something to do with all of these. This God reveals himself primarily in the events of our personal, family, tribal, national, and world history, in terms of persons, their relations, and their destinies.

Second, we note that *God encounters us in time.* Yet because God is Lord over time, the unity and purpose of past, present, and future are found in his will. Consider the lonely traveler, Jacob. Overtaken by darkness, he stops for the night in a barren spot. He falls asleep, and dreams that heaven touches earth by means of a great stairway, and that God's messengers are busily coming and going on errands for the Heavenly King. But the vision is only to prepare Jacob for the word, and the word which comes to Jacob is a remarkable one. It comes personally addressed from One who knows him, and it ties together his past, present, and future. It begins with the past: "I am the LORD, the God of Abraham." The ancient promise first given to Abraham and Isaac is now renewed point by point to Jacob. But that is not the end of the matter. God does not encounter us in terms of the past alone, for if he did, our parents' religion would never become our own, and our interest in it would never be more than an antiquarian pursuit or an exercise in nostalgia. The moment has to come when what we have heard from those who have gone before takes hold of us personally, calls us, transforms our lives.

So something new is added to the promise, just for Jacob. "I am with you" (present tense), "and I will keep you wherever you go and I will bring you back" (future tense). Past, present, and future are united in the overarching purpose of God. To encounter God in time means that life in this present moment suddenly makes sense when we discover that he prepared the way for us in the past and that he charts the course for our future. No corner of our life is hidden from him. His care extends beyond our view, whichever way we look. With the Psalmist we say:

> Lord, thou hast been our dwelling-place in all generations,
> Before the mountains were brought forth
>   or ever thou hadst formed the earth and the world,
> From everlasting to everlasting thou art God.
>   (Ps. 90:1–2)

That means that when I have dug as far as I can dig into the past, God is already there. When I have projected as far into the future as I can see, God is already far beyond that point, beckoning me onward with the assurance that the whole sweep of history is under his controlling purpose. "From everlasting to everlasting" means as far as I can see in either direction—and beyond! God's purpose guarantees the future.

33

God's purpose for Jacob, and through Jacob for the world, is not going to be thwarted, not even by Jacob's scheming, conniving tricks, or the difficulties into which they will later lead him. God has spoken, and he will bring his word to fulfillment. God is Lord of time.

Third, we learn that *God encounters us in space, at certain places.* "Jacob left Beersheba and went toward Haran. And he came to a certain place, and stayed there that night" (Gen. 28:10–11). "A certain place" seems to be a very ordinary place, a bare and windswept place, full of rocks and sky, somewhere between Beersheba and Haran, a place where the securities of home are left behind and the uncertainties that lie ahead press in on the lonely traveler. Just a place where darkness happened to overtake him. Surely it was not a place in which Jacob expected to meet the God of his ancestors, and not the spot at which heaven and earth came closest together! Just "a certain place."

But it was a definite and particular place, a point on the map. Jacob set a large stone up on end to mark the spot. He poured oil on the stone to set it apart as a holy place. He could come back to it later, and did (Gen. 35:1–15). He brought his family years later on a pilgrimage and pointed to the stone and said, "Right there is where it happened!"

Of course it could hardly be otherwise if God is really to encounter us in history, for our history is made up of particular times and places. If we are to meet God at all, it has to be at some particular time and place. But what an amazing fact is this "scandal of particularity" in biblical religion, that God comes to us at a particular point in human history, a particular intersection of time and space.

This place is never the same again, of course, after God has met us there. That spot where Jacob slept, which had previously been just "a certain place," now becomes Beth-El, "the house of God," a holy place, a sanctuary. It becomes a pilgrimage site. People come seeking the God who once appeared there. They sleep there, hoping to hear his voice in their dreams.

What a risk God takes by entering the particularities of our lives! Perhaps someone will cry out, "Stop the clock!" Then history will come to a standstill, crowds will converge on the spot and build a magnificent shrine to enclose the holy space, and people will henceforth go there to find God. If it happens in our day, television crews will arrive. Newspapers will report about it. Travel agents will book tours to visit the shrine. Hotels will spring up around it. How could

God's voice ever be heard again over all that commotion? God wishes to speak to us somewhere, so he takes the risk that the somewhere will then become the "only-where," and that what should have been a memorial stone will become an object of adoration, an idol.

Fourth, we learn from this story that God reveals himself to us where he will. Jacob thought that he had left God behind, back in Beersheba. He now learns that God is not tied down to that or any place. Jacob cannot leave God behind; he is going along ("I am with you . . . and will keep you . . . and will bring you back."). There is no need for Jacob to stay at Bethel contemplating that stairway to heaven or hoping to hear God's voice there again. He might as well get up and move along. For it is on the way that we are suddenly surprised to find heaven touching earth, in this place or that. We were not seeking it, perhaps, nor expecting to find it, but there it is! God surprises us by revealing his presence where we least expect it. He is the God of our journey, the God of our wanderings "to and fro upon the earth." And if we ask, "Where, exactly, is he to be found?" the answer is, "Where he wills to be found."

Finally, we learn from Jacob's story that God encounters us as the people we are—sinful and on the run. Jacob is not cleaned up and on his best behavior. There is no thought of his deserving this revelation or even preparing for it. He is not acting pious or praying. He is in flight! He has left home under a shadow, fleeing from the consequences of an act of deception. He is a troubled traveler with an uneasy conscience. He faces a night of fitful sleep. His pillow is a stone. But God chooses to reveal himself to this person. Perhaps this is the most important lesson: that God will reveal himself to a schemer like Jacob, enter into relationship with him, place him in the line of the promise, and announce his intention to use him for his purposes. What a God this is who will work with such a person as this! This story gives hope to all spiritual descendants of the schemer Jacob. If God had not been willing to work with Jacob, we remind ourselves, then he might pass us by also.

PATRIARCHAL RELIGION AND MOBILITY

The lack of attachment to holy places is related, of course, to the mobile kind of life which the patriarchs lived. After all, Abraham is depicted as a *ger*, a sojourner or resident alien in the land. But he is also pictured as moving from place to place (". . . and Abraham journeyed on," Gen. 12:9). Whether there is a seasonal pattern to these moves is not made clear. Finally he pitches his tent at Mamre, near Hebron, and that becomes his principal place of residence (Gen. 13:18), but his moving around does not end (20:1). During his so-journ in Canaan he is found at Shechem, Bethel, Mamre, in the Negev between Kadesh and Shur, in Gerar, at Beersheba, and, for a time, in Egypt. Thus Abraham is a tent-dweller who moves about from time to time. The same is true of Isaac and Jacob. Although each has his place of primary residence (Beersheba for Isaac, Shechem for Jacob), each also moves around with his flocks and herds, and shuns the Canaanite cities. While it may not be correct to call them pastoral nomads, there is no question about their mobility in the stories of Genesis.[14]

This mobility formed the background for patriarchal religion, and it figured in the set of circumstances to which the religion was rele-vant. But that mobility did not create the people's faith! Not every-one who moved around and lived in tents in the second millennium B.C.E. in the Fertile Crescent had a faith like the faith of Abraham and Sarah, Isaac and Rebekah, Jacob, Leah, and Rachel. But the kind of life that they were living when the revelation came to them did shape the character of their faith. Patriarchal religion is stamped with the characteristics that we have discussed, and these same characteristics were taken up into subsequent forms of biblical religion.

This matter of the mobility of the patriarchs has been illuminated, in recent years, by the discovery, in documents of the second millen-nium from Mesopotamia, Asia Minor, and Egypt, of groups of people called *Habiru*. Enough has been learned about them to show that there are interesting parallels between their way of life and that of the patriarchal clans of the Bible.[15] The predominant view is that these *Habiru* form a social class, not a people or ethnic group.[16] They are described as outsiders having no citizenship in the established cul-tures, living on the fringes of society somewhat like modern gypsies or transient workers. They frequently appear as marauders, conduct-ing "guerrilla attacks" against cities or caravans, pillaging and plun-dering on their own. At other times they hire themselves out as mercenary soldiers and occasionally end up as prisoners of war, pressed into forced-labor projects. An Egyptian text speaks of some *Habiru* slaves employed to carry stones in quarries.

There are certain analogies between what is said about the *Habiru* and the situation of the biblical Hebrews.[17] Both groups are strangers, not fully integrated into the societies in which they live; both are mobile and widespread. The times and places in which they appear sometimes correspond.

Like the *Habiru*, the patriarchs pitch their tents on the edge of the territory of Canaanite city-states, or of Egyptian or Philistine cities. They also resist becoming closely related to those societies. Only Lot in Sodom is an exception, and we see what happened to him as a result (Gen. 13:8-13; chap. 19)! When Jacob's family is invited to settle down in Shechem, the basic incompatibility between them and the inhabitants of that city produces a violent separation in which the sons of Jacob plunder Shechem (Gen. 34:27-29), exactly as the marauding *Habiru* do in the extrabiblical texts.

This does not mean that the *Habiru* and the patriarchal clans are identical. It suggests, rather, that this element of the population in the ancient Near East may form the larger background out of which the ancestors of the tribes that we know as Hebrews originally came. If so, this enhances our understanding of the mobility of the patriarchal clans and the part which that mobility played in their religion. Just as it was true for the *Habiru*, so it is for the patriarchal groups that connection with particular places was incidental, ambiguous, and transitory.

HOLY PLACES

A number of places are mentioned in the patriarchal stories which have significant connection with the religious traditions. They are *holy places*. How did this come about and what are we to make of it?

This question is illumined by considering the way in which the patriarchs and their religion encountered the inhabitants of the Canaanite cities with their religion. As the patriarchs moved into the land and came into contact with the sanctuaries of the Canaanites, their religion acquired an interest in those holy places. Many of the sanctuaries mentioned in Genesis were clearly known as holy places before the patriarchs arrived. These places now became associated with an event in the life of one of the patriarchs (e.g., Abraham's divine visitors at Mamre, Genesis 18), or a cultic action of one of the patriarchs ("there he built an altar to the LORD," Gen. 12:7, 8; 13:18;

22:9; 26:25; 35:7; also, with a different verb, 33:20; 35:1, 3). In effect, this represents the claiming of that holy place—in the name of the God of the patriarch.

But this does not change the basic character of patriarchal religion. The adoption of those holy places does not bring along with it the way of understanding those holy places which rules Canaanite religion. Rather, these places are taken up into the story of the personal relationship involving the patriarch, his clan, and the God who calls them and promises them a future.

SUMMARY

We have seen that patriarchal religion holds many things in common with its ancient religious environment. But it has four distinct features which seem to set it apart: (1) emphasis on personal relationship with God; (2) the voluntary quality of that relationship; (3) centrality of the word; (4) focus on time, especially the future created by the promise. This group of features moves the religion of the patriarchs and matriarchs along a different path from that taken by the religions of the surrounding peoples.

When we compare these characteristics with Abraham's faith (chap. 1), we see that the two are quite compatible. All the patriarchs and matriarchs, in fact, are sojourners like Abraham. They are resident aliens with no permanent attachment to their places of residence. Their religion is centered in time and history more than in space and nature—on the move into a promised yet unknown future. They have heard the call of God, have responded to that call in faith and obedience, and are living out their lives on the basis of that word from God, within the relationship to which that word invited them.

As we move on, we must ask: To what extent does the picture just described prove consistent with the faith of the tribes united later under the name "Israel"? Is patriarchal religion a genuine forerunner for the faith that emerges from the exodus and the period of Moses? For an answer, we turn to the Book of Exodus.

— 3 —

MOSES,
EXODUS, AND
WILDERNESS WANDERING

WHEN WE MOVE from Genesis 50 to Exodus 1, we discover that a long time has passed since our last glimpse of Joseph and his brothers. The descendants of Jacob who now meet us in the first few paragraphs of the Book of Exodus are a different group of people from the families of Jacob's clan that had once settled their flocks in the area called Goshen by invitation of the pharaoh (Genesis 46). Their fortunes have also changed radically, for Egypt is now a very different place.

In spite of that jump in time, the literary transition between Genesis and Exodus is quite smooth. The listing of Israel's sons who had come down to Egypt and the repeated references to Joseph at the beginning of Exodus (1:1–8) would not be enough, by themselves, to accomplish this smooth transition. It is also the assumption that the same God is at work in both stories, as stated explicitly in Exod. 2:24 and repeated many times afterward, which makes us feel that the connection between the two books is not an artificial one. Prior to Exod. 2:24, God appears briefly to reward the midwives (Exod. 1:17, 20, 21), then disappears during the briefly sketched story of Moses' birth and growth to adulthood (1:22—2:22). Only when we come to 2:24 is God clearly identified as the God of the ancestors of the previous book: "And God remembered his covenant with Abraham, with Isaac, and with Jacob."

A new theme and an old one come together to cement the connection between the events of Genesis and those of Exodus. The new theme is suffering. The descendants of the patriarchs "groaned under their bondage, and cried out for help, and their cry under bondage came up to God" (Exod. 2:23). The old theme is that of the covenant which God had made with their ancestors. The connection between the two is made by the verb "remember": "God remembered his covenant." But the remembering is triggered by the suffering and the resulting cry: "God heard their groaning and God remembered."

The God who is now about to intervene on behalf of these Hebrew slaves is identical with the God of the patriarchs and matriarchs of Genesis. This is stressed again in the story of Moses' call (see Exod. 3:6, 13-17), and the subsequent narrative. But there is another question which needs to be faced if we are going to read Genesis and Exodus as one continuous story. That the God of the exodus is identical with the God of the patriarchs flies in the face of a problem: the God of the exodus has a different name (Yahweh) from the names for the deity that appear in many of the Genesis stories (El, Elohim, El Shaddai).

This fact is faced in the story of Moses' call, when Moses queries the One who has spoken to him as follows:

> If I come to the people of Israel and say to them, "The God of your fathers has sent me to you," and they ask me, "What is his name?" what shall I say to them? (Exod. 3:13)

The new name is revealed:

> God said to Moses, "I AM WHO I AM" [or "I WILL BE WHAT I WILL BE"]. And he said, "Say this to the people of Israel, 'I AM has sent me to you.'" (Exod. 3:14)

The connection is made:

> God also said to Moses, "Say this to the people of Israel, 'The LORD [YHWH][1] the God of your fathers, the God of Abraham, the God of Isaac, and the God of Jacob, has sent me to you': this is my name for ever, and thus I am to be remembered throughout all generations." (Exod. 3:15)

Henceforth, this One is to be known as YHWH (the LORD), the God of your (or our) fathers (3:16). It is usually assumed that the form YHWH in 3:15 ("Yahweh"; see n. 1) is a third-person singular form of the Hebrew verb "to be," or "to become," which the preceding verse uses in the first-person singular.[2]

The reiteration of the call of Moses in Exodus 6 brings the change in divine names in the Priestly (P) and Elohist (E) sources into clearer focus:

And God said to Moses, "I am the LORD [YHWH]. I appeared to Abraham, to Isaac, and to Jacob, as God Almighty [*El Shaddai*], but by my name the LORD [YHWH] I did not make myself known to them." (Exod. 6:2–3, P)

This change in names is obscured when the English versions offer "God Almighty" as the translation for *El Shaddai* and "the LORD" for YHWH, the name revealed to Moses. People who have grown up in a monotheistic environment, accustomed to the use of various synonyms for "God" in religious settings, will read the words "LORD" and "God Almighty" without being aware that different proper names stand behind these translations, unless they happen to read an explanatory footnote in their Bible. They may even wonder at the discussion about a change of names in Exodus 6.

The smoothness of the transition from the patriarchal names for God to the new name revealed to Moses is not just something introduced by modern translations, of course. Theological unity is already assumed by those who put these stories together; we see it in the use throughout the book of what had become a general term, *elohîm* ("God"), even when a divine name is not being proclaimed or discussed (Exod. 1:17, 20, 21; 3:4, 13a, 14a, 15a).

But this examination of the fusion of names raises more sharply than before the question I posed at the end of the first chapter. Does patriarchal religion "fit" well with the religion which emerges from the exodus event and the period of Moses, or are they really quite different religions? For we must not suppose that originally, in that polytheistic environment, it could have been merely a matter of "playing around" with different names for the deity.

The stories in Exodus 3 and 6 suggest that the name YHWH is here being revealed to Moses and his people for the first time. Historically this must surely be correct. At the same time, the assertion by the Yahwist source (J) that YHWH is the same God who was active from the very beginning (Gen. 2:4; 4:26) is theologically correct. By using that divine name in the story of creation in Genesis 2, the author of J is saying, "The God whom we know as the LORD

41

(YHWH) is the same God who created the world and who called our ancestors." But the other narrative sources, by reserving the name YHWH (the LORD) until the time of Moses' call, are adding, in effect: "But we did not know him as the LORD (YHWH) until he revealed that name to Moses." My point is that this new name first comes into view in conjunction with the new event of revelation—the exodus from Egypt—and that this name was not known to the patriarchs.

Thus it seems clear that it is not enough, in order to unify the events reported in Genesis with those which follow in Exodus, merely to state that the God named X and the God named Y are identical. It is also necessary to look at the events through which the nature of YHWH becomes visible, and then determine whether or not we can really affirm that this is the same God as the God of Abraham, Isaac, and Jacob. From the standpoint of the religious traditions in question, one must ask whether patriarchal religion in Genesis is a genuine forerunner of the faith of the exodus and the Sinai covenant. We expect some differences, of course. The religion of the exodus traditions moves in a different world and, to some extent, breathes a different atmosphere. So we do not look for uniformity, but for evidence of genuine continuity.

THE CALL OF MOSES (EXODUS 3)

The nature of exodus/Sinai religion is clearly seen in the story of the call of Moses (Exodus 3—4), which can be viewed as a paradigm or model for the whole story of Israel's life with God which unfolds in the following chapters and books.

1. As the scene opens in Exodus 3, Moses is pasturing the flocks of his Midianite father-in-law Jethro in the Sinai wilderness, near the base of a sacred mountain. Startled by the sight of a bush which is on fire but is not consumed, he draws near for a closer look, and is even more startled to hear a voice which seems to come from the bush, calling out, "Moses, Moses!" The One who speaks knows his name, and in the dialogue which follows, also reveals his own name. Thus we see from the very first moment of this encounter that the faith of which this story speaks has to do with a personal relationship. Moses' personal identity is established by God, and in what follows, Moses is invited into a relationship with the One who calls.

But it is not Moses alone who is being called. In him and through him, the whole people to which he belongs is being called. The covenant[3] which is later established between the LORD and the Hebrews when they come to Sinai is an intensely personal relationship (Exodus 19—24). At its core, the covenant is a relationship of love and loyalty on the LORD's side (Exod. 19:3-6), and of trust and commitment on the side of the Hebrews (Exod. 24:3). Precisely because Israel is called to exclusive loyalty to one God ("no other gods," Exod. 20:3), this relationship is inclusive. In polytheism, each of life's many areas is assigned to a different deity. But in the exclusive relationship with one God which is being established here, every single area of life is subject to that God's rule.

There are important differences between the Sinai covenant and the patriarchal covenant to which we shall return later. But at this point, notice that both speak of a personal relationship and both use the word "covenant" to describe that relationship.

In that ancient world all relationships could be described in one of two ways: either in terms of kinship or of covenant. Kinship terminology could be used literally and realistically by some religions to describe the relation between a people and their gods. In Israel this was impossible. Israel could not think of itself as physically descended from or related to the LORD. It was a bold, even daring, poetic metaphor that Hosea (eighth century) used in speaking of Israel as the LORD's bride (Hosea 2) or even his child (11:1-4). But such figures of speech could never be understood literally. In Israel, the only viable option was to speak of the relationship to the LORD as some kind of covenant. The alternative would have been to abandon the language of personal relationship altogether, and this Israel could not do. Israel knew that this relationship to God was an intensely personal one.

This led Israel to speak of God's actions in colorful, passionate language that some have labelled anthropomorphic. It is anthropomorphic language, of course, but as George Ernest Wright pointed out, anthropomorphic language is greatly to be preferred over the alternatives—in Israel's world and ours.[4] Human beings (*anthropoi*) have no choice but to speak of God by analogy, using human life as the source of metaphors, since none of us speaks "God-language," and we would not be able to communicate anything to our fellow humans if we did. "Covenant," then, indicates that the God-human

43

relation is a personal one, but Israel's poets go far beyond the limits of covenant language in describing the intense relationship between Israel and the LORD.

2. Next comes a gracious invitation which the LORD extends—an offer of help. There is nothing compulsory or coercive about this relationship. It is voluntary on both sides.

The LORD, moved solely by love and compassion, has decided to rescue this enslaved people (Exod. 3:7-8). They are invited to believe the promise of salvation sent by the intermediary, Moses (4:30-31), and later to enter a covenant with the God who has rescued them (19:5; 24:3, 7-8). By choosing to do so, they will commit themselves. The covenant relationship, entered voluntarily by both parties, has for Israel both inner, moral force and the potentiality for life-giving, life-enhancing growth. No longer externally bound, these former slaves bind themselves to the compassionate God who has taken pity on their weakness and distress.

From the standpoint of a later age (eighth–seventh centuries), this voluntary quality of the covenant partly accounts for the hearing that the prophets received from a rebellious people who did not really want to listen to their message. It even helps account for the fact that the prophets survived. In spite of their disobedience, the people recognized that what the prophets were saying was rooted in the covenant. Had they not heard and even repeated, in the annual covenant renewal ceremony, the words which their ancestors had spoken at Sinai: "All that the LORD has spoken, we will do" (Exod. 34:3)?[5]

3. From beginning to end in this story, speaking and hearing are prominent. Dialogue is the mode of this encounter and this revelation. It is the Word which is of primary importance. Visionary elements are insignificant by comparison. The burning bush serves only to get Moses' attention. Once God begins to speak, the bush is forgotten (Exod. 3:4-21). Even the visual phenomena at the mountain later on (Exod. 19:16-20) serve only as prelude to the words which God will speak there.

The Hebrew word *dabar* has a wider meaning than its usual translation as "word" would indicate. It is also translated "matter," "event," "affair," and sometimes even by the colorless word "thing." Even when it means "word," there is more implied for the ancient Israelite than our use of "word" might suggest.[6] For the word that is truly spoken comes out of the heart which conceives it and carries with it something of the very being and purpose of the speaker. Words are active and powerful. Once spoken, they have an effect that cannot be reversed. Words are incipient deeds, and deeds are words carried to their proper conclusion. The will of the speaker moves through word to action. There is no gap between word and deed. An understanding of the dynamic character of the Word is essential for comprehending the Bible.[7]

Thus when we speak of the priority of the word, we include the act of God which is inseparable from that word. This is seen in the close correspondence between the *messages* to Moses which announce in advance what the LORD intends to do on behalf of this people and the *events* in which those announced intentions are carried out. It is also seen in the role of Moses as the mediator of both word and deed. The act by which God intervenes on behalf of this suffering people is not just a bare happening with no meaning. That event is a rescue *from* one situation *to* another, a saving act *by* someone *for* someone. It is not just a lucky escape, or an accident, or the inevitable and automatic consequence of economic or political or social causes. What it means is announced in advance when God speaks to Moses and the people and tells them that he has heard their cry, has seen their distress, and has decided to "come down and deliver them out of the hand of the Egyptians and to bring them up out of that land to a good land" (Exod. 3:7–8).

The deed by which God rescues them follows the word. The word (message) makes clear God's motive for doing this deed and the purpose he has in mind. The word reveals God; it shows who he is. It shows that this word/deed is not an isolated, discrete, meaningless happening, like "acts of God" in insurance-policy language. God also has no intention of rescuing these people from bondage only to leave them stranded on the eastern shore of the sea, wondering what to do next. The word makes it clear that this act of God's is the beginning of something—a relationship, a destiny, a future.

Just as the word must become flesh in the deed, so the act of God requires the word if what happens is to be meaningful. Therefore the word *precedes* the event but it also *accompanies* it every step of the way, and then *follows* it in every remembrance and liturgical celebration of the event forever afterward.

This interlocking of word and deed requires the presence of a mediator through whom God communicates the word and makes clear its connection to the deed.[8] In this case it is Moses. His presence is essential to the story. The people are repeatedly confused and rebellious. The event alone does not communicate its meaning to them. It is not self-evident.

> "What have you done in bringing us out of Egypt? Is not this what we said to you in Egypt, 'Let us alone and let us serve the Egyptians'? For it would have been better for us to serve the Egyptians than to die in the wilderness." And Moses said to the people, "Fear not, stand firm, and see the salvation of the LORD; for the Egyptians whom you see today, you will never see again. The LORD will fight for you, and you have only to be still." (Exod. 14:11-14)

The intimate linkage between word and act is not limited to this story of the exodus. It is a recurring element of the biblical drama: God's word and God's deed are always inseparable! The story of Moses' call is a model for the life of Israel, and in this story the priority of God's word is clear.

4. This encounter and the religion which grows out of it are primarily focused on time rather than space, on history rather than nature. Such focuses make this faith radically different from the other religions of the ancient Near East.

Of course the history which now comes into view goes beyond the limits of family and clan history which we saw in Genesis, into the larger arenas of tribal and national history. The stage is enlarged, but the basic concerns are the same. Between the day on which the LORD announces his intention to rescue this people and the day on which that announcement is fulfilled, two points on a line are plotted and historical continuity is established. God has announced in advance what he is going to do. When he has done it, the people to whom it was announced look back and say, "He has done what he promised to do." They also look forward and say, "The things of which he has spoken in the future will surely come to pass."

The past of this history also has greater depth now. It goes all the way back to the patriarchal stories: "I am the God of your father, the God of Abraham, the God of Isaac, and the God of Jacob." So there are now four points by which to plot the trajectory of the line of this history: the time of the promise to the fathers, the moment of the promise to Moses, the time of the fulfillment of certain promises, and the goal toward which other promises, not yet fulfilled, still lead.

The center of gravity, however, does not lie in the past. As with Abraham, so here, it is the future which is the center of interest. The word of personal address which lies at the heart of this invitation is a word of promise. It points toward a future and moves toward it; it creates that future. At the same time, it is a word of command. The invitation to relationship necessarily includes that dimension (see chap. 1). Every relationship of life (parent-child, sister-brother, friend-friend, employer-employee, wife-husband) has a shape, a definition, a set of requirements without which that relationship would cease to exist.

When the LORD invites the recently liberated Hebrew slaves into a covenant, that relationship has to be defined and described. The "Law of the covenant" does that. It is a continuation of the gracious deed by which God redeemed this people from slavery that he now proceeds to make plain to them what life in covenant with him will be like. They are not left in doubt as to what their God expects of them. He gives them the Torah[9] as a guide to instruct them in the way they are to walk as his covenant partners.

Both as demand and promise, the Word of God creates a future. Just as Abraham could not see where his call would lead, so it is not possible for the Hebrew people at Sinai to see where this relationship will lead. But they can see what kind of God this is, and they take the risk of committing themselves to him. There is no relationship without risk. But without the relationship, there is no future!

THE SACRED MOUNTAIN

The importance of the mountain in the exodus story might seem to call in question this alleged priority of time. But the stress on time does not mean that the Bible has no concern for space, any more than the stress on history means that it has no concern for nature. Space, too, falls under the LORD's dominion, and any revelation which is genuinely historical must "take place," not only at specific times but also at specific places.

High mountains were commonly regarded as holy places in the ancient world, and the awesome peaks of the Sinai peninsula had probably been regarded that way long before Moses and his people came to encamp at the foot of one of them. The surprising thing here is the relative lack of importance attached to the location of Mt. Sinai itself. Emphasis on the historical event has become the primary thing. There is no suggestion that the people must remain here to build a permanent sanctuary, or return here to worship the LORD. Nor is there any solid evidence for the practice of pilgrimage to the mountain. The lone journey of Elijah to Mt. Horeb (1 Kings 19) must be seen as unique rather than exemplary. So little were the people of God interested in the exact location of the place itself that Judaism preserved no memory of it. Traditions that attempt to mark the location of Mt. Sinai stem from Christian sources which begin some fifteen hundred years after the time of Moses, in the third century C.E.

ABRAHAM/MOSES

We can now return to our original question and affirm that in spite of obvious differences of time and circumstance, there is an affinity between patriarchal religion and the religion of exodus/Sinai which is concerned with more than peripheral matters. Patriarchal religion is a genuine forerunner of the religion of Moses and his people. The religion of the patriarchs was already moving away from the other religions of that world, and along the same pathway which is now taken by the exodus/Sinai covenant faith.

The call to Abraham and the call to Moses both serve as a model for the call to the children of Israel. Abraham hears God's voice and responds in faith to the word of promise and command. He embarks on a journey into the unknown, trusting solely in the One who has called him. Cut loose from all other securities, he lives by the promise, and on the basis of that faith moves into the future. With the very same words we might well describe the "many" in Egyptian bondage and the "one" who is called to lead them out. Moses and his people, like Abraham, are called out of the land in which they live, away from reliance on the false gods of Egypt, to a new relationship based on trust in the One who had called them. Just how difficult it is for a people who have been slaves to break out of that physical and mental servitude is illustrated by the problems which Moses experiences with them, both before their departure and after they are in the wilderness. Internal liberation takes much longer to accomplish than external deliverance!

SOJOURNER

The Book of Exodus makes little use of the Hebrew word *ger* ("sojourner"; see chap. 1) to describe Israel's status in Egypt. When Moses makes that word part of the name of his first son, *Ger*shom, saying "I have been a sojourner in a foreign land" (Exod. 2:22), he is referring to the land of the Midianites in which he dwells. But later theologians often speak of the Hebrews in Egypt as sojourners, whether by way of narrative anticipation (Gen. 15:13) or later reflection (Deut. 26:5). Perhaps they do so because Abraham's descent to Egypt in earlier days was spoken of that way (Gen. 12:10) and because they view his experience as a prototype for that of his descendants. As early as the legal document called the Covenant Code (Exod. 20:23—23:19), Israelites are enjoined to take special care for the sojourner in their midst because of their own experience in Egypt (Exod. 22:21; 23:9). This concern is frequently expressed in the legal material which later forms a part of the book of Deuteronomy (Deut. 10:18-19; 24:17-22).

THE WILDERNESS PERIOD

The new life of trust in the LORD to which the liberated people have been called is now illustrated in stories of their wilderness wanderings (Exod. 15:22—19:1; Num. 10:11—14:45; 20; Josh. 1—3). To the LORD alone they must look for (1) guidance and protection (the pillar of cloud and pillar of fire), (2) food and drink (manna, quails, water from the rock), and (3) the fulfillment of the promise (safe arrival in the Promised Land). The wilderness period, which is extended to a full generation because of their disobedience, becomes a period of training and discipline. Three religious institutions of Israel which the story associates with this period illustrate the unique nature of this faith.

The Two Shrines

Two of these institutions should be examined together. They are the covenant shrines at which encounter with the LORD takes place after the people have left Sinai: the Ark of the Covenant and the Tent of Meeting.[10] Each of these shrines demonstrates that this religion is not attached primarily to holy places. Each is portable. The tribes do not have to return to a certain place to find the LORD. The LORD will go with them, just as he went with Jacob when he left Beersheba. This is specifically stated in Exod. 33:14: "My presence will go with you, and I will give you rest." The Ark and the Tent are symbolic focal points for the realization of this promise of presence.[11] To stand before the Ark is to stand before the LORD who is invisibly enthroned above it. The Tent is folded up and carried along on the journey, and wherever it is pitched again, determined by the moving cloud of the Presence, the LORD himself "comes down" to meet his people in the person of their leader Moses, and later, Joshua.

In each case, the nature of the shrine corresponds to the relationship-centered nature of this faith. It is the personal encounter with the LORD, ever happening anew, that is the powerful center of this religion. And the LORD accompanies them as they are "on the way." They do not have to call a halt to the historical march in order to meet their God. Their God is on the road with them! They walk in God's presence as they journey, for it is God's word and will which provide the power and purpose for that journey.

Of so little importance are the resting places along the way through the wilderness that scarcely one of them can be identified with any assurance today. Judaism has never shown any interest in locating them, or in building shrines or markers on the spots. This relative lack of attachment to holy places is an integral part of biblical faith. This faith is born in the context of historical existence, and in that matrix it grows and develops, far removed from those religions which are engaged in a "flight from history."[12] The God of the Bible goes along with his people, and if they want to find God, they must go along, too, for their going is his doing. It is God who first revealed the road and set them on their way, and it is God who goes with them.

The Sabbath

The third religious institution which Exodus traces to this early period is the Sabbath.[13] The story in Exodus 16, which connects the giving of the manna with the Sabbath, makes two things clear.

1. The observance of the Sabbath rest is intimately connected with trust in the LORD and obedience to his command. The LORD's gift of manna sustains life. Yet the gift itself is not to be grasped or clung to; only the Giver is. Just as Abraham was not allowed to idolize the child

of the promise, so the children of Israel in the wilderness must learn that the gift of life comes by the LORD's word of promise. The moment they put their trust in the gift and ignore the command of the Giver, then that which had been the means of life turns into a foul-smelling picture of death: "It bred worms and stank" (Exod. 16:20 KJV).

Deuteronomy gives a later theological interpretation of the manna. Jesus of Nazareth at his temptation quotes Deuteronomy on the relation between life and faith: "that human beings do not live by bread alone, but by every thing [word] which proceeds out of the mouth of the LORD" (Deut. 8:3, quoted in Matt. 4:4).

Sabbath observance, then, is linked with the persistent theme we have noticed all along: God alone is God! Trust is to be placed in God alone. No other foundation for life is to be seized, counted on, or clung to. Not even God's good gifts may be elevated to the status of a foundation for life. A relationship with God can only be one of radical trust and obedience.

2. The Sabbath illustrates yet another aspect of biblical religion we have seen: the priority of time. This religion is mainly concerned with the sanctification of time, not space, and of this fact the Sabbath is a principal symbol and institution. Abraham Heschel points out that in the account of creation, the first time the word "holy" (qadosh), the word most intimately connected with the divine, is used, it is applied not to any object in space, but to time: "And God blessed the seventh day and made it holy."[14]

Thus three major religious institutions with roots in the wilderness period—the Ark, the Tent of Meeting, and the Sabbath—reveal a faith whose character is parallel with that of the faith of Abraham, Isaac, and Jacob. The story of the exodus, the Sinai covenant, and the wilderness sojourn confirms this connection at every point.

=4=

LIFE IN
THE LAND
OF PROMISE

THE PROMISE OF land was one of the basic ingredients of the patriarchal stories, alongside the promise of blessing and abundant offspring.[1] It is first introduced in Gen. 12:7, becomes a major theme of the Abraham stories (Gen. 13:14-17; 15:7-20; 17:8), is reiterated in the stories of Isaac and Jacob, and becomes one of the themes that ties together the narrative that runs from Genesis to Joshua.

SETTLEMENT IN THE LAND OF PROMISE

In the outline of this "history of salvation" which we find in Deut. 26:5-9, the last item—"and he brought us into this place and gave us this land, a land flowing with milk and honey" (v. 9)—represents the final stage of the story which began with the "wandering Aramean" ancestor.[2] From Deuteronomy's point of view, the taking of the land of Canaan still lies in the future (Deut. 26:1). Thus at the end of the Torah (Pentateuch), the people have not yet entered the land. Moses has been given a view of it from the top of Mt. Nebo east of the Jordan River, but he cannot enter it (Deut. 34:4). So he dies and is buried in the land of Moab.

Critics have often puzzled over the fact that the last stage of the Salvation History falls outside the Torah itself.[3] At the end of the Pentateuch, the promised land remains a promise. Only in the book of Joshua is the tension resolved. This leads many to assume that the old narrative sources now embedded in the first four books of the Bible must have had an ending which brought the story to a conclusion by telling of the entry into the land, and that one or more of these endings is now to be found in the first chapters of Joshua, or even in Judges 1. Nevertheless, the fact remains that at the end of the Torah as we have it, all eyes are strained toward the promised land, eagerly awaiting the fulfillment of the promise. The biblical story is powerfully oriented toward the future.

Once the people have crossed the Jordan River (Joshua 3), the process of occupying the land of Canaan begins. That process is not completed until the time of David, when most of the remaining Canaanites are finally dominated and assimilated into his united kingdom. But their incorporation into the state does not necessarily mean that they have abandoned their old form of religion. In the centuries that follow, growing syncretism threatens the very foundations of Israelite faith. A life-and-death struggle ensues between Yahwism and Baalism. In the course of this struggle, the true nature of faith in the LORD becomes more fully and sharply defined as its adherents become self-consciously aware of the deep incompatibility between the LORD and Baal. They see that the covenant and its stipulations touch every area of life because the LORD demands their exclusive loyalty. Prominent among the questions that have to be faced is that of the land.

In the transition from the life of the wilderness to life in Canaan, problems related to agriculture—fertility of soil, adequate rainfall, avoidance of hail, locusts, and other pestilences—pose a new set of questions for those Hebrews who had been rescued from Egypt and sustained in their struggle for survival by a God associated in their minds with the mountains and the desert.[4] "Is the LORD, the God of exodus and Sinai, ruler over this land as well? Does the soil and its cultivation fall under his domain, or ought we to consult with the Canaanites and their gods for matters pertaining to crops and cultivation? After all, they have been at it for a long time," the Israelites may have thought and questioned among themselves.

There is little doubt that the Israelites absorbed agricultural information from the Canaanites and at the same time borrowed many of their seasonal agricultural festivals. There is also no denying the fact that the Israelites were strongly tempted to slip Baal into their religious framework alongside the LORD (Yahweh for politics and war, Baal for crops) or to attempt a merger of the two, blurring the distinctions between them. The struggle over this issue is one of the factors

53

that called forth the efforts of the great prophets of Israel from Elijah to Jeremiah.

TWO QUESTIONS

In relation to the land, this long struggle can be looked at from the perspective of two questions. The first is: Who is really the God of this land, and of the whole area of life which the land represents (nature and creation)? This question is gradually answered throughout the story of Israel. The conflict about it does not come to a final conclusion until the fall of the two kingdoms and the exile (721, 586 B.C.E.). But the answer is really present, of course, at the heart of the exodus/Sinai tradition, and most succinctly in the first command-ment of the Decalogue: "You shall have no other gods before me" (Exod. 20:3). This claim for the LORD's uniqueness, with its demand for exclusive worship from Israel settles this question in principle. But many centuries must pass before the full implications of that principle are thought through, reflected upon, and internalized by Israel.

The LORD, God of exodus and Sinai covenant, of wilderness wanderings, and of the conquest of the land, finally comes to be clearly and unequivocally identified as Creator and Lord over na-ture as well as history. The steps in this theological process can still be discerned here and there, although the story seems to assume that its conclusion was clear from the beginning. The power and claims of Baal and of all other gods are gradually broken. The culmi-nation of this development is reached when the undisputed, solitary dominion of the LORD (YHWH) over all creation is proclaimed in language of unparalleled beauty and sublimity in Isaiah (chaps. 40—55) during the exile of the sixth century B.C.E. (Isa. 42:5-17; 43:9-20; 45:18-19). But there were many in Israel who had seen and believed for generations before the emergence of that prophet of the exile that it was the LORD alone who governed all things, not only his-tory, but also land and its fertility, sun, moon and stars, wind and rain, rivers and seas. The Priestly Hymn of Creation (Genesis 1), which states this belief without equivocation, had been under devel-opment for a long time before it reached its final form during or after the exile. So the question, Who is the God of the earth and sky and universe? is in the process of being answered all the way from Sinai to the exile.[5]

The second question is, in a way, more difficult: What does it mean to be the people of the LORD in the promised land, and how are the people who live in covenant with the LORD related to the land? Under Joshua, the people called Israel take possession of the land. The LORD gives it to them and they receive it as an inheritance from Abraham and their other ancestors who held it, not in deed but by promise. The land is divided among the tribes, clans, and families, each receiving a portion of the inheritance (Joshua 13—19). The ancient promise of the land has been fulfilled. But the question still remains: How will the covenant people view the land, now that they occupy it?

First, they must remember that the promise of the land is conditional. This is spelled out repeatedly and in great detail:

> But you shall keep my statutes and my ordinances and do none of these abominations . . . lest the land vomit you out, when you defile it, as it vomited out the nation that was before you. (Lev. 18:26-28; see also 26:27-34; Num. 14:30; Deut. 11:13-17; 28; 29:22-28; 30:15-20)

The people of the LORD do not possess the land in any absolute sense. They have not always lived in this land. They remember when they came and under what circumstances. Furthermore, their occupancy is conditional. The land belongs to the LORD (Josh. 22:19: "the LORD's land"). They dwell in it, cultivate it, enjoy its fruits and render thank-offerings to the true Owner, by whose gracious will they are allowed to hold the land in trust (Deut. 26:1-11).

Some of the consequences of this attitude toward the land are displayed in the story of Naboth's vineyard (1 Kings 21). In this story the social and economic implications of the conflict between Israelite and Canaanite religions come clearly into view. The unique attitude toward the land which grows out of the Sinai covenant is shown to be in irreconcilable conflict with a view of political power which grants absolute authority to the human ruler and ignores the rights of the humbler members of society. This story demonstrates the prophets' understanding of life in covenant with the LORD, and comes from the prophetic circles which preserved and interpreted the history.

But is this view of the land held by only a small circle of prophets? In the time of the kingdom(s), do the Israelites as a whole continue to think of themselves as sojourners in the land, like Abraham, or is that concept a part of the patriarchal past which they have left behind? Do they remember the contingent character of their relation to the land once they "possess" it?

ISRAEL'S RESPONSE TO THE QUESTIONS

It is not possible, of course, to know how every individual Israelite thought about such matters. But for Israel as a whole, it seems that the answer to the last two questions is no. This negative answer is based on three considerations: (1) the use of the word "sojourner" (*ger*) and of the Abrahamic model during this period; (2) general observation of the difficulty of holding on to such a concept of contingency in human affairs; (3) the protests and accusations of the prophets.

1. A study of the occurrences of *ger* and related words shows that the Israelites did not apply that word to themselves in this period and did not think of themselves as any longer belonging to that category. In the past, in Egypt, they had been sojourners (*gerim*). This is often mentioned as the motive for the laws which require them to treat the sojourners among them with justice and kindness: ". . . for you were sojourners in the land of Egypt . . ."; "you know the heart of the sojourner" (see Deut. 10:19; 24:17–18; Exod. 23:9; Lev. 19:33–34). Even this degree of identification with the *ger* is surprising, for most nations did not remember their beginnings in such an unflattering way.[6]

Nevertheless, that was an unhappy experience which they are glad to have left behind. *Ger* is a negative concept in the language of this period. It is an unpleasant thing to be a miserable *ger*. Nowhere does that word seem to be a positive symbol for the life of the descendants of the *ger* Abraham. In fact, by an interesting reversal, it is the descendants of those very people among whom the patriarchs had once sojourned, the Canaanites, who are now called "sojourners." This shows that the term is still being used in its original, sociological sense of "resident alien." It has not yet been interpreted metaphorically within a theological frame of reference. That will come later.

That the Israelites do not apply the word *ger* to themselves in this period may prove only that they have not yet engaged in enough reflection on the patriarchal stories to begin to apply them to their own lives as metaphors. With or without the word *ger*, then, the question persists: Do the Israelites of this period live within the Abrahamic pattern? Is that a functioning model for Israel's life under the monarchy? The answer is yes and no. Israel is called, does respond in some ways, and does live in covenant with the LORD. But as generations come and go, and it becomes increasingly clear what a life of complete trust and obedience to the LORD demands in all the circumstances to which a nation is subject, it also becomes increasingly evident that Israel is not living in complete dependence on the LORD alone, but is bowing down before a great many idols.

2. Observation of human behavior, in general, suggests that it is unlikely that a group of people who occupied a territory with the belief that God had long before promised it to their ancestors would then think of themselves as anything other than the rightful owners of that land. There is no longer any reason for them to think of themselves as temporary occupants or resident aliens in a land belonging to others. The land now belongs to them! The idea that it belongs to the LORD who graciously permits them to occupy and use it is likely to evaporate because of our human tendency to assume that the LORD can always be counted on to favor his people with unqualified support and protection.

It is not likely, therefore, that the contingent nature of Israel's occupancy of the land will be kept in mind. Human beings have difficulty in considering any possession conditional. This universal tendency is accentuated in Israel during the time of the monarchy by two factors.

First, concentration of power and wealth in the hands of a royal bureaucracy and a growing class of urban merchants and landholders backed by state power brings with it a changed understanding of "land" which is in conflict with the tribal ideals that dominated Israel's earlier days. Such tribal views of land more closely approximate those of modern Bedouin clans. A family may have a claim to a piece of land at the place of its longest residence during the year and may even raise crops there. Or the family members may barter for the use of such a piece of land. But they also traverse and use a great deal of other land which is clearly not theirs in any sense of individual ownership. It may be the territory of their clan, and the clan will fight to keep outsiders away. But it is a communal possession of which each family makes use in a variety of ways.

The transitions made by the Israelites between the eleventh and the eighth centuries B.C.E., from a society of independent tribes to a royal state, and from a predominantly agricultural economy to one dominated by trade and the concentration of wealth and property in urban centers, produce a shift *from* the communal view of land *toward* the idea of individual ownership.

A second factor in the life of Israel which works against remembering the conditional nature of the promise of land is the existence within the Israelite covenant traditions themselves of a tension over the very nature of the covenant. This tension centers on whether the covenant is contingent or not.

There are many covenants in the Bible, but the covenants between God and his people can be divided into two basic types: the Abrahamic-Davidic type and the Mosaic-Sinaitic-Deuteronomic type. In the Abrahamic-Davidic covenant traditions, the relationship between God and his servant is viewed as one of gracious promise, which is initiated by God and bestowed upon the human recipient, who is not under obligation to fulfill any stated conditions for the continuance of the covenant in force.[7] In the Mosaic-Sinaitic-Deuteronomic stream of tradition, on the other hand, the covenant, while no less the result of divine love and favor, is understood as involving certain requirements for the human party which are spelled out and essential for the covenant's continuance. These stand alongside the obligations which the divine sovereign voluntarily takes upon himself.[8]

This Sinaitic type of covenant is regarded by many scholars as the normative one for Israel, while the Abrahamic-Davidic type is seen as supplementary at best, or a complete perversion at worst. Such a view is a distortion of the evidence, however, encouraged by the circumstance that we read most of the story of the early history through the spectacles of its final editors, the Deuteronomistic historians, who are committed to the Sinaitic tradition.[9] A more accurate assessment is that each of these covenant theologies is legitimately rooted in the ancient traditions and each is an equally valid expression of covenant faith. The theology of Israel, and of the Christian church as well, develops within the tension between these two ways of understanding the divine-human covenant.[10]

But each of these ways of understanding the covenant has its own built-in danger. Sinaitic covenant theology with its emphasis on human obligation, when carried to extremes, tends toward legalism. Abrahamic covenant theology, with its lack of specific stipulations, tends to denigrate the law and fall into the sin of overconfident presumption. These two types of covenant theology correct and balance each other, if they are held in constant tension. But either one, cut off from the other, slides toward a perverted understanding of the relationship to God and results in disaster for the life of God's people.

During the time of the Davidic dynasty in Jerusalem, a covenant theology was developed which undergirded the royal house and the preeminence of Zion and its Temple. It built upon the promises given to David by the LORD as recorded in 2 Samuel 7, and counted on the unqualified continuance of those promises in perpetuity, without reference to the behavior of the human parties. The model for that royal covenant seems to be the earlier covenant with Abraham, to whom David is related by a number of interesting circumstances.[11]

The promise of land is originally associated with the Abrahamic covenant, and is frequently found together with the Hebrew word *leolam* (usually translated "forever" or "everlasting"; see Gen. 13:15; 17:7, 8, 13, 19). This is a key word in both Abrahamic and Davidic covenants. Just as the LORD promises David a royal house and a descendant sitting upon his throne "forever" (2 Sam. 7:13, 16, 29), so the promise of the land to Abraham's descendants was "forever." Thus the place which the land occupies within the framework of covenant thinking makes it vulnerable to those temptations and tendencies to which the Abrahamic-Davidic type of covenant is particularly subject. It tends to become part of a noncontingent, permanent claim which Israel has, or presumes to have, upon God, quite independent of any fulfillment of stipulations on Israel's part. It is to this dangerous tendency that the prophets speak.

3. The preexilic prophets deliver the LORD's message to a people who have forgotten the covenant and have forsaken the LORD's instruction. Which covenant have they forsaken?

It is clear that the preexilic prophets are calling the people to account on the basis of well-known, clearly defined requirements, that is, the Mosaic-Sinaitic-Deuteronomic understanding of covenant (see Hosea 4; Amos 2:6–8; Jer. 7:8–11). So serious have their violations of the covenant's requirements become, say the prophets, that the covenant itself is in danger of being destroyed (Hos. 1:9). The danger to which the Abrahamic-Davidic covenant theology was especially susceptible has now manifested itself in the life of the people. The fixed, eternal, noncontingent promises to Abraham (and David) have become objects of trust and bulwarks of confidence. People think that it simply does not matter how they live with respect to the requirements of the Sinaitic *Torah*. God's election of David and of Zion will stand "forever." The LORD's presence in the Temple guarantees the security of Jerusalem (Jer. 7:4).

Even Isaiah of Jerusalem, the prophet most deeply influenced by the theology of the royal House of David, announces God's coming judgment because the nation has abandoned the type of stipulations set forth in the covenant of Sinai (Isaiah 1; 5). When Isaiah announces that Jerusalem will be spared from an Assyrian attack (ca. 701 B.C.E.; see Isa. 37:33–35), this is a message of salvation for that particular historical crisis, not a guarantee of permanent protection for Jerusalem. But the latter is exactly what the popular theology had made of it by the time Jeremiah arrived on the scene a century later. People believed that Jerusalem could not fall, and probably quote Isaiah to support that conviction (Jer. 5:12–13; 6:1–8; 26:7–11).

In their bold, uncompromising presentation of the LORD's claims on Israel, the eighth and seventh century prophets attack every idol—every object in which people place their trust other than the LORD alone. Most of all, they warn against placing trust in the very gifts and promises of their gracious God, and the misuse of those gifts as obstacles rather than aids to faithfulness. Every institution of religion is attacked when the people rest their confidence in the mere possession of holy things and holy places (Zion, Mic. 3:9–12; the Temple, Jer. 7:1–15), or in the proper performance of the prescribed rituals (sacrifice, Isa. 1:10–20; circumcision, Jer. 4:4), or even in the possession of the scroll of the Torah itself (Jer. 8:8).

The same thing holds true of their attitude toward the land. People believe that the promise of the land means that they can never be removed from it. It is a part of the package known as "the sure mercies of David." The prophets' denunciations show how far people have strayed from understanding that the land is a gift from the LORD contingent upon their fulfillment of the requirements of the covenant.

> For if you truly amend your ways and your doings, if you truly execute justice with one another, if you do not oppress the alien, the fatherless or the widow, or shed innocent blood in this place, and if you do not go

after other gods to your own hurt, then I will let you dwell in this place, in the land that I gave of old to your fathers for ever. (Jer. 7:5-7)

Drastic measures are called for to put things right. Israel has backslidden so far from the Sinai covenant that some of the prophets (Hosea and Jeremiah) can speak with fond remembrance of the wilderness period when the covenant was still new. This does not mean that the wilderness period and its way of life had become an "ideal" for Israel.[12] Rather, it means that things had gotten so bad in eighth and seventh century Israel that those prophets saw a need for the rebellious nation to undergo once again a discipline like that of the wilderness period before reentry into the land. They also used the language of the wilderness period as poetic metaphor for the "stripping down" which the coming judgment would bring with it. But no one ever suggested that they go back to the wilderness and stay there. Such an idea would be contrary to the basic thrust of biblical faith, which is oriented toward the future, not the past. Even when they were in the wilderness, the people had survived the rigors and dangers of that time only because they had hope in the future which God had promised. The wilderness was not the goal toward which God was leading them. Their experience there was not meant to last forever.

There was something positive about Israel's "honeymoon" with the LORD at Sinai (Hos. 2:14-15.; Jer. 2:1-2): the exuberant, total devotion of a new relationship of love and trust. There was also something positive about the wilderness period: the necessity laid upon Israel to learn to trust fully in the LORD and in the LORD alone. But the wilderness did not create this, and a return to the wilderness would not restore it. It was part of Israel's relationship with God as defined at Sinai, and it could only be restored if they would heed the prophet's message and return to the LORD who was calling them to repentance.

Thus it is clear from the message of the prophets that Israel is not living in accord with the Abrahamic pattern. People have embraced one side of the Abrahamic saga: they see themselves as inheritors of unconditional and eternal promises. But they do not see themselves as descendants of Abraham as sojourner, uprooted from false securities, separated from all idols, and living by faith and hope alone. They do not pass the test which Abraham passed when he resisted the temptation to cling to the gift of the promised child rather than trust the Giver and his promise (Genesis 22). They do not inherit the promise as promise; they try to grasp it as a possession. Had this succeeded, of course, they would have brought the forward move- ment of the promise to a halt; they would have ceased to have a future. The Israelite of the kingdoms clings to the Abrahamic promise but does not live by the Abrahamic vision.

Thus we could say that the preexilic prophets denounce God's people for failing to walk in the sojourner-tradition of Abraham, that is, for failing to live a life of radical trust and obedience. The LORD's decision, they announce, is that all of the false supports for life, all of the idols in which the people have put their trust, are to be removed; or rather, Israel is to be removed from them, insofar as exile can accomplish such a removal. Then the LORD will see whether Israel, deprived of their idols, will return to their God or whether they will make new idols for themselves to replace the old ones.

The final blow falls in 586 B.C.E. The Babylonian army lays siege to Jerusalem for the second time in a dozen years. The walls are finally breached, the city is burned and plundered, the Temple looted and destroyed. Surviving inhabitants who have not managed to escape are rounded up by the pagan soldiers to begin the long trek to Babylon with the words of the prophet Jeremiah still ringing in their ears.

> Your ways and your doings have brought this upon you.
> This is your doom, and it is bitter;
>   it has reached your very heart.
>
> (Jer. 4:18)

═ 5 ═

SOJOURNERS
ABROAD
AND AT HOME

THE PEOPLE OF GOD once again find themselves sojourners in a strange land—this time the land of Babylon. Once they were
sojourners in the land of Egypt; now (586 B.C.E.) they again dwell
among a people of foreign speech and pagan religion. The question
for Israel in exile is clear: Has the LORD cast his people off forever? Is
there any hope, any future for the people of Israel?

The answer to that question must come from the LORD. Ezekiel
makes this clear when he is shown, in a vision, a valley of dry bones
representing the fallen host of Israel (Ezekiel 37). "Son of man, can
these bones live?" the Lord asks him. "Lord, thou knowest," the
prophet replies. Ezekiel certainly does not know the answer. He
knows that he cannot bring those bleached bones back to life. Nor
can Israel itself provide a future. Only the LORD can do that.

The logic of the Mosaic-Sinaitic-Deuteronomic covenant theology
(see pp. 58–59), rigorously applied, would lead to the conclusion that
the story of Israel with the LORD is finished. The covenant relationship depended for its continuance upon fulfillment of the obligations
assumed by both parties. The LORD had been faithful but Israel had
not, despite repeated warnings sent through messengers over the
centuries. One concludes, therefore, that the covenant is dissolved.
Israel has broken it. It seems clear that most of the exiles had come to
just that conclusion.

What kept Israel alive during that dark hour? It was God who
kept them alive then, just as he had in the past, by his word coming
into their history at this time of crisis through certain groups and

individuals who became the mediators of that word in this new situation. But what is there in the faith which they have inherited that can serve as the foundation of hope for a future?

COVENANT HOPE

Some basis for hope could be found in each type of covenant theology (see chap. 4). The Mosaic-Sinaitic-Deuteronomic covenant theology could lead to despair, but need not necessarily do so. Hosea had already shown another way of interpreting it, in the eighth century, before the fall of the Northern Kingdom. In the depths of despair, Hosea announces the annulment of the covenant: "And the LORD said, 'Call his name Not my people, for you are not my people, and I am not your God'" (1:9). The covenant is broken!

But that is not the end of the story. The prophet discovers, through his own tragic personal experience, that the covenant can be restored:

> And in that day, says the LORD . . .
> I will have pity on Not pitied,
>   And I will say to Not my people,
>   "You are my people";
> and he shall say, "Thou art my God."
>   (Hos. 2:23;
>   see all of 2:14–23)

A clue to this dramatic reversal is given in Hosea 11.

> When Israel was a child, I loved him,
>   and out of Egypt I called my son. . . .
> How can I give you up, O Ephraim!
>   How can I hand you over, O Israel! . . .
> My heart recoils within me,
>   my compassion grows warm and tender.
> I will not execute my fierce anger,
>   I will not again destroy Ephraim
> for I am God and not man,
>   the Holy One in your midst,
>   and I will not come to destroy.
>   (Hos. 11:1, 8–9)

When the covenant relationship has been destroyed, Israel must remember the nature of the God who rescued a helpless slave people from Egypt at the first. If, as Deuteronomy insists, the covenant was established in the first place solely on the basis of God's love for this people (Deut. 7:7–8), then perhaps there is a basis for hope in what Hosea has learned about God's undying love. Maybe that love goes deeper than Israel's sin. Maybe God will not let Israel go, but even now will act with compassion, as at the beginning, to rescue and restore this fallen people. It depends completely upon the LORD. The question is: Is it God's will to take Israel back?

The Mosaic-Sinaitic-Deuteronomic covenant theology could lead to the hopeful asking of this question, but that of the Abrahamic-Davidic covenant could go further and provide a confident answer. God had made sure promises to David and to Abraham. These promises carry the key word "forever." God will not fail to carry out his word of promise (Jer. 33:17–26).

Thus it is still possible to have hope, even in exile, with Jerusalem lying in ruins. The word of God is still heard. It still creates a future toward which God's people may look and move.

WHY DID IT HAPPEN?

At this point, another problem presents itself. In the light of those "sure mercies of David," those unconditional promises about Zion and the royal throne, how is it possible to understand the terrible catastrophe that has happened? Zion was destroyed and the Temple lies in ruins.

To deal with this question, the Sinaitic covenant theology is essential if the faith of this people is to survive. A meaningful future is possible only if it can be made plain why this tragedy has befallen Israel, and how this stands in agreement with God's previous self-revelation.

The preexilic prophets (e.g., Amos, Hosea, Micah, Isaiah, Jeremiah) had prepared the way. Typically they presented their messages with a two-part structure: an announcement of judgment was joined with a clear statement of the grounds for that judgment (see, e.g., Amos 5:10–11; 6:4–7).[1] It only remained for the Deuteronomistic historians to apply that prophetic method retrospectively to the whole course of the nation's history as it moved toward the tragedy of 586. This catastrophe did not occur because the gods of Babylon were more powerful than Israel's God. On the contrary, an amazing and unheard-of thing has happened. Israel's God, far from being the pawn of his worshipers, at the service of their national claims and

65

interests, has gone so far as to punish his own people for their sins and to use the army of another nation as the instrument for carrying out this punishment. The judgment itself corresponds to those announcements of judgment repeated so often in the prophets' messages. The history of the kingdoms, compiled and interpreted by the Deuteronomistic historians,[2] provides the grounds for that judgment and corresponds to an indictment in a legal proceeding. The history displays the sins of the nation for all to see.

One other important question about the judgment remains. For what kinds of sins had God punished them? For not bringing to the sanctuary the right offerings on the right day in the duly prescribed manner? For cultic infractions like these Israel's neighbors would have expected punishment from their gods. Amos speaks to this question on behalf of all the preexilic prophets.

> I hate, I despise your feasts,
> and I take no delight in your solemn assemblies.
> Even though you offer me your burnt offerings and cereal offerings,
>   I will not accept them,
>   and the peace offerings of your fatted beasts
>   I will not look upon.
> Take away from me the noise of your songs;
>   to the melody of your harps I will not listen.
> But let justice roll down like waters,
>   and righteousness like an everflowing stream.
>
> (Amos 5:21-24)

In Israel, it is for failure to execute justice and maintain righteousness, for breach of the covenant and its obligations, that judgment comes. There is no quarrel with ritual practice, but there is a quarrel with those who think that by going through the motions of the ritual, they can satisfy the LORD's requirements. In the view of Israel's prophets, the sins of the nation are primarily moral, not ritual. They can be summed up in general terms as sins against the LORD, as "turning away." At root, they come from lack of trust and obedience. Ritual activity cannot take the place of faithfulness to the covenant.

This theological interpretation of the fall of Judah, based on the Sinaitic covenant, makes it possible to go on believing in the righteous will of the holy God and promises to make life in a restored community worth living. Thus both types of covenant theology prove to be essential for the continued existence of Israel as the people of the LORD.

THE SOJOURNER DURING AND
AFTER THE EXILE

With rare exceptions, the Israelites who lived during and after the exile do not apply the word "sojourner" (ger) to themselves. That is not particularly surprising in light of the development that had taken place in the use of the term.

Originally, as we have seen, the sojourner was a resident alien living in a land not her or his own, and having no native rights. In Israel, certain legal and social rights developed for the sojourner, inspired by the memory that Israel had once been one in Egypt. The sojourner enjoys the same legal protection as the native Israelite, for example, the right of asylum (Num. 35:15; Josh. 20:9), and protection from oppression, along with the widow and the orphan (Exod. 22:21; 23:9; Deut. 24:14; Lev. 19:33, 34). The fruits of the sabbatical year are available for sojourners as much as for others (Lev. 25:6). They may share in the tithe of the Levite, along with widows and orphans (Deut. 14:29), and in the gleanings left in the fields and vineyards for the poor (Deut. 24:19; Lev. 19:10; 23:22). It is even possible for a ger to become rich. A native Israelite may sell himself to a ger as a hired servant (Lev. 25:47ff.). The laws of Deuteronomy never tire of upholding the rights of the sojourner. They are to receive equal justice before the judges (Deut. 1:16); their justice is not to be perverted (Deut. 24:17). The LORD loves the sojourner; Israel must do the same (Deut. 10:18, 19).

Sojourners also take part in most of the worship activities of Israel. Like everyone else they must observe the Sabbath (Exod. 20:10; Deut. 5:14), the Day of Atonement (Lev. 16:29), and the renewal of the covenant (Deut. 29:11). They are to hear and obey the reading of the Torah at the Feast of Booths (Deut. 31:12). They may offer a burnt offering to the LORD (Num. 15:14), and when they do so, "there shall be one statute for you and for the stranger who sojourns with you. . . . As you are, so shall the sojourner be before the LORD" (Num. 15:15). The sojourner participates in the Feast of Weeks (Deut. 16:11), and is invited to keep the Passover to the LORD, just as the Israelite does (Num. 9:14). This seems to mean, according to Exod.

67

12:48, that they may eat of it when all the males of their household have been circumcised. Circumcision, then, is the one barrier that might keep the sojourner from full participation in the cultic life of the community. Once this barrier is passed, the sojourner is no different from the native Israelite, as far as participation in religious worship is concerned.[3]

Of all the prophets, Ezekiel was the most influential on the priestly architects of the restored community in Jerusalem after the exile. Ezekiel's vision of the apportionment of land in the new Israel provided for equal treatment of the sojourner.

> So shall you divide this land among you according to the tribes of Israel. You shall allot it as an inheritance for yourselves and for the aliens who reside among you and have begotten children among you. They shall be to you as native-born children of Israel; with you they shall be allotted an inheritance among the tribes of Israel. In whatever tribe the alien resides, there you shall assign him his inheritance, says the LORD God. (Ezek. 47:21-23)

The postexilic priestly legislation moves toward eliminating all distinctions and incorporating the sojourner fully into the religious life of Israel. On the whole, the priestly laws are specifically said to apply to the sojourner equally as to the native Israelite (Lev. 16:29; 17:8, 12; 18:26; 20:2; 24:16, 21, 22; Num. 15:30; 19:10). Thus the *ger* is one who was not born a Jew, but has been fully converted and assimilated into the Jewish faith.

Because of this major shift in the understanding and use of the Hebrew word for "sojourner," a study of that word's occurrences would not be a sufficient guide in our search for the followers of the Abrahamic model of the sojourner. The word *ger* is traveling in a new direction. This provides a clue as to why Israelites living *after* the exile did not normally apply that word to themselves. But in spite of that fact, we discover that some of God's people do begin to apply the term to themselves during and after the exile. The evidence comes from a variety of sources.

During the Exile

Second Isaiah (Isaiah 40—55) makes extensive use of the story of the exodus from Egypt and the journey through the wilderness to Canaan as a prototype for the release and return from exile which he announces, in the LORD's name, to his fellow captives in Babylonia. He draws figures of speech and religious types from the old story to describe the coming great event, which will be superior to the former one in every way (Isa. 52:12; 54:9-10; 55:3, 12; 43:18-19).

This analogy between exodus from Egypt and release from Babylonian exile requires his first hearers and us to assume also an analogy between the sojourn in Egypt and the sojourn in Babylon. Just as their ancestors had once been in Egypt, so now are they, in the Land of the Two Rivers. Second Isaiah makes that analogy explicit in the one passage in which he uses the word *ger* for the sojourn in Egypt and then compares that to the situation of his fellow exiles (Isa. 52:4-5). We are justified, therefore, in assuming the same analogy elsewhere, even when the word *ger* is not used. The situation of the exiles, like that of their ancestors in Egypt, is one in which they hear God's word addressed to them in their misery and despondency, calling them to trust in the LORD for deliverance, and to hope for the future which he has in store for them.

The prophet Ezekiel does not make such extensive use of exodus typology, but he does speak plainly of the exile as a sojourning:

> I will bring you out from the peoples and gather you out of the countries where you are scattered, with a mighty hand and an outstretched arm, and with wrath poured out; and I will bring you into the wilderness of the peoples. . . . I will purge out the rebels from among you, and those who transgress against me; I will bring them out of *the land where they sojourn*, but they shall not enter the land of Israel. (Ezek. 20:34-38; my italics)

Ezra 1:4 also speaks of the Jews in exile as "sojourning" in the various places in which they live. Thus we see that it is possible for the Jews to apply the word *ger* to themselves once again, during the exile. But when they do so in these passages, it is clear that they are returning to the original sociological and legal meaning of the word.

The Return and Restoration

A few years after the preaching of Second Isaiah, return and restoration begin. After Cyrus, ruler of the Medes and Persians, had conquered Babylon, he issued an edict in 538 B.C.E. permitting the return of exiles to Jerusalem. In the decades that followed, more than one caravan expedition was organized to return. The total number of people involved was not large. After all, most of the exiles belonged to the second generation in Babylon. They were well settled there, living conditions were not difficult, the journey back to Jerusalem was dangerous and costly, and conditions in Jerusalem far from ideal. Only the most courageous and hardy among them would undertake such a trip. Once back in Jerusalem, they had to work out relations with the descendants of those who had remained in the land, and begin the slow and difficult task of rebuilding—first, houses to live in, then the Temple. The defense walls around the city had to wait.

As we read the story of the restoration in Ezra-Nehemiah, it becomes clear that a change has taken place in these people. The conditional character of their covenant with the LORD is now taken very seriously. No longer are the gifts of God's grace taken for granted as they had been before the exile. The preaching of the earlier prophets, preserved in written form by their disciples and driven home by the somber events of recent decades, is now taken seriously. People are concerned about faithful obedience to God's holy will. This disposition to cling wholly to the LORD underlies the determination, in the postexilic community, to organize all of life in a thorough-going and all-embracing network of civil and religious structures that will, as far as possible, shut out the unclean and forbidden and shut in the believing and the faithful.

The absence of walls around Jerusalem symbolizes the openness and exposure of its community to paganism and the kind of religious syncretism which had hastened its downfall in the past. In 444 B.C.E. a Jewish layman named Nehemiah, highly placed in the Persian court, asks and receives permission from his king to journey to Jerusalem for a term as governor (Neh. 2:1-8). Once there, he vigorously sets about the task of building walls: both the literal, physical walls around the city, and the inner, mental and spiritual walls which he sees as necessary to protect the integrity and even the existence of the people of the covenant (Neh. 2:11-30; 13). The religious side of this program is carried further by Ezra, priest and scribe, who returned from Babylon with a copy of the Book of the Law of God and set about to bring life in the Jerusalem community into conformity with that book (Nehemiah 8—9).[4]

If these efforts at times tended to produce a certain rigidity and exclusivism that ran the risk of erecting new idols in place of old ones, that was certainly far from the intention of Ezra or Nehemiah. Nor does it match the self-understanding of the Chronicler, whom we can discover marching into the Temple in a noisy and joyous procession of worshipers, jubilantly praising the LORD and exalting his glorious name, so that it might be honored throughout the whole earth (2 Chron. 29:25–36). These children of Abraham are trying with all their strength to take the holiness of God and what he requires of Israel with total seriousness. If, in seeking to do God's will, they risk making their actions into new foundations for life, it is because of the difficult role to which the sojourner is called. The universal tendency is to fashion one's own foundations for life which will take the place of radical trust in the One who calls us into relationship with him.

The builders of the postexilic community in Jerusalem are keenly aware of the dangers of paganism on the outside and the tendency toward disobedience and rebellion on the inside. With the word of God before their eyes, on the written scroll and in the lessons of historical experience, they labor to build a community in which God's will can be carried out in every area of life. No longer is the conditional character of the covenant forgotten!

A New Use of "Sojourner"

Our third line of evidence brings us back to the word "sojourner" (*ger*). In the light of its history, it is surprising to find a few passages from this period in which the word is used in reference to the relationship of the people of God to the land and to the LORD himself, rather than in its sociological or legal sense.

> The land shall not be sold in perpetuity, for the land is mine; for you are strangers and sojourners with me. (Lev. 25:23)

This passage from the Holiness Code (Leviticus 17—26)[5] sets forth the law for the Year of Jubilee. Every seventh year, the land is to be allowed to rest and enjoy its sabbath. But after seven times seven years, the fiftieth year is to be celebrated as the Year of Jubilee. Not only does the land rest during this year, but the land that has been sold during any of the previous forty-nine years now reverts to the family which originally received it as an inheritance. "Each of you shall return to his property and each of you shall return to his family" (Lev. 25:10). It was not the land itself that had been sold, but the use of it for a certain number of years, or the harvests that remained from the date of sale to the Year of Jubilee.

Verse 23a summarizes the principle: "The land shall not be sold in perpetuity . . ."; verse 23b gives the reason: "for the land is mine; for you are strangers and sojourners [gerim wetoshabim] with me." The LORD is the owner of the land. To his people he entrusts the use of it.

Often in biblical Hebrew, as in any language, a concept like that of the sojourner is not limited to a single word, but is part of a semantic field. It will have several companion words, some so close in meaning as to be virtually synonymous, others somewhat more tangential. At times, two such words combine to form what is virtually a single idea. For example, the word ger is connected by the conjunction we ("and") to the word toshab. The toshab (from the verb yashab, "to sit, stay, dwell") is less permanent than the ger, less assimilated, with no house of his own. But when the two words are joined, they merge into one total meaning. Translators must try to capture the total idea of the Hebrew word pair by using two English words that are similarly related. The favorite English translation of this word pair is "strangers and sojourners." This does not mean that "strangers" translates the first word gerim (pl. of ger) and "sojourners" translates the second word toshabim. It simply means that the English word pair attempts to capture the total idea of the Hebrew word pair.

> But who am I, and what is my people, that we should be able thus to offer willingly? For all things come from thee, and of thy own have we given thee. For we are strangers before thee, and sojourners, as all our fathers were; our days on the earth are like a shadow, and there is no abiding. (1 Chron. 29:14–15)

Here David and the people have just made a great offering of provisions for the Temple which is to be built by David's son Solomon, and they rejoice, "for with a whole heart they had offered freely to the LORD . . ." (29:9). David then prays an offertory prayer (a source for offertory sentences still in use today). The theme of this prayer is that everything which they have given really came from God in the first place (29:14). Then follows the clause, "For we are strangers before thee, and sojourners, as all our fathers were."

Here we find the same word pair used in Lev. 25:23, "strangers and sojourners" (*gerim* w*etoshabim*). In Leviticus, a theological understanding of life before the LORD and of the land undergirds the legal principle of the Year Jubilee. Here, in the context of worship, the same words express an attitude, not just to the land, but to everything in life. The LORD is exalted as head above all (1 Chron. 29:11), and the words "strangers and sojourners" take on a similar breadth of meaning. They describe the true status of God's people; they express a totally accurate self-understanding.

The words, "as all our fathers were," could be understood as referring to all who had gone before, but more likely they have the patriarchs in view, since the word *ger* is especially associated with them in the old stories. In fact, the scene which comes to mind is the one in which the aged Jacob has made the long trip down to Egypt to be reunited with his son Joseph, long thought to be dead. Joseph brings his father in for a brief audience with the pharaoh of Egypt, and in response to the pharaoh's polite inquiry about his age, Jacob replies:

> The days of the years of my sojourning are a hundred and thirty years; few and evil have been the days of the years of my life, and they have not attained to the days of the years of the life of my fathers in the days of their sojourning. (Gen. 47:9)

The patriarchs are sojourners for their whole lifetime. Therefore, the whole of life is a sojourning!

The work of the Chronicler (ca. 400 B.C.E.), inaugurates the tendency to look back to the patriarchs and other figures of the past as heroes and models for the faithful. This tendency will become more prominent in the centuries to come.

> Hear my prayer, O LORD, and give ear to my cry;
> hold not thy peace at my tears!
> For I am thy passing guest,
> a sojourner, like all my fathers.
>
> (Ps. 39:12)

Psalm 39 is generally thought to have originated after the exile. Here the very words which 1 Chron. 29:15 used to express the proper assessment of God's people as they stand before God are used by an individual petitioner as the basis on which she hopes that her prayer will be granted. The word pair "passing guest/a sojourner" (*ger w^etoshab*) express her complete dependence upon God and her sense of identification with the ancestors who stood under God's protection and promises. This worshiper clings, in complete trust, as they did, and prays to be treated as they were.

The close similarity between Ps. 39:12 and 1 Chron. 29:15 raises the question of the possible dependence of one passage on the other. If there is such a dependence, it seems most likely that the Chronicles passage is the basis for the psalm verse, for it is not just in the verbal similarity of this phrase that they are related. In 1 Chron. 29:15b we read, "Our days on the earth are like a shadow, and there is no abiding." These words find more than an echo in Psalm 39; they are the subject of reflection and further development.

> Lord, let me know my end,
> and what is the measure of my days;
> let me know how fleeting my life is!
> Behold, thou hast made my days a few handbreadths,
> and my lifetime is nothing in thy sight.
> Surely everyone stands as a mere breath!
> Surely each goes about as a shadow!
> Surely for nought are they in turmoil;
> they heap up, and know not who will gather!
>
> (39:4–6)
>
> . . . surely everyone is a mere breath!
>
> (39:11d)
>
> Look away from me, that I may know gladness,
> before I depart and be no more!
>
> (39:13)

It is the brevity and transience of life on earth that intensifies the psalmist's suffering and sharpens her spiritual crisis to an almost unbearable point. Here we have moved one step further in the process of interpretation that became evident in 1 Chron. 29:15. The sojourning of "the fathers" in the land of Canaan has become the symbol for the sojourning of the people of God, and an individual among them, upon the earth. But the symbol of the sojourner is reinterpreted in such a way that the sojourning of the patriarchs themselves is now seen in a new light. Their sojourning is now viewed not only as a sojourning in the land of Canaan but also as a sojourning before God upon the earth. Here we have moved toward the metaphorical interpretation of the sojourner that we encounter in later Jewish and Christian writings.

I am a sojourner on the earth; hide not thy commandments from me. (119:19)

Thy statutes have been my songs in the house of my pilgrimage [m^{e}gûre]. (119:54)

The references here are briefer, with few clues to the way "sojourner" and "pilgrimage" are understood. The context deals with the study of the Torah, and provides no clear clue to the meaning such as we found in Psalm 39 and 1 Chronicles 29. It is possible that here, too, we are dealing with a metaphorical understanding of sojourning.

In these four passages, we find theological reflection on what it means to call Israel, and the individual Israelite, a sojourner. Here, for the first time, God's people explicitly see themselves as "strangers and sojourners" before the LORD in a land (or earth) that belongs to him. They are his guests, and their stay is brief. With confidence they look to the LORD on whom everything in life depends.

$=6=$

THE CENTURIES
BETWEEN
MALACHI AND MATTHEW

THE PERIOD FOLLOWING the Chronicler's work (ca. 400 B.C.E.) saw the end of the Persian Empire and the arrival of Greek rule in the lands of the East. It was a difficult period of ferment and change for all the peoples who fell under the conquering might of Alexander the Great and the Hellenistic civilization which he propagated. For the Jews, these new influences challenged the traditions out of which they lived and inevitably affected the ways in which they understood and expressed their faith. Our information comes mostly from the large body of Jewish literature which overlaps chronologically with the last books of the Hebrew Bible and the early Christian writings. The term "intertestamental literature," widely used for this literature, is inaccurate and there is no consistency in the limits assigned to it. In this chapter, I am speaking of approximately the last three centuries B.C.E. and the first two centuries of the Common Era. There are many important factors in these centuries which have a bearing on the theme of the sojourner, and to them we now turn.

JEWISH LIFE AFTER 586 B.C.E.

After the fall of Jerusalem in 586, with the accompanying deportation of exiles, Judaism was found in two contexts: (1) the Jewish community in Jerusalem and the surrounding area; (2) the other Jewish communities scattered throughout the world in "Diaspora" (Greek for "Dispersion"). The experience of living in Dispersion is the experience of the majority of Jews in the centuries following the exile. Life and faith develop in the Diaspora with an inward and an outward focus.

The Inward Focus

This focus is aimed at preserving the community and the traditions, at teaching and reinterpreting the Sacred Writings, and at developing institutions that will strengthen and nurture the life of faith. People ask, What does it mean to be the people of God in continuing "exile" from the Promised Land? How do we define and identify ourselves? How are we different from those among whom we live? How do we structure and carry on worship without the Temple? How can we be faithful here to all that God has taught us? How can we "sing the LORD's song in a strange land?" (Ps. 137:4).

The Outward Focus

This focus has to do with relations to the pagan culture of the Persian Empire and, later, to that of the Hellenistic cities of the Greco-Roman world in which these Jews of the Diaspora lived. A primary issue is that of separation versus assimilation. How can the faith inherited from the past be preserved and sustained in the face of pagan pressures? Unless resisted, the subtle, eroding influence of Hellenistic culture with all its attractiveness would finally result in the undermining of the Jewish faith, and complete assimilation. This conflict is felt, of course, not only in the Diaspora, but in Jerusalem itself, as the Maccabean Wars and the Books of Daniel, Judith, and 1 and 2 Maccabees demonstrate.

One result of the struggle over such questions is the clear rejection and ridiculing of all forms of idol worship in the Jewish literature of these centuries. (See, e.g., *The Letter of Jeremiah* as well as *Bel and the Dragon* in the Apocrypha.) That the issue of separation was a part of Abraham's call out of the idolatrous, polytheistic culture of Mesopotamia (see chap. 1) had been seen for a long time. It could now be articulated anew and indeed *had to* be, if his descendants were to live as true children of Abraham in the pagan world out of which he originally came.

Thus another result of the struggle is the growing sense among some Jews of alienation from the pagan culture and rejection of its values. This is the movement toward separation from the pagan world. At the same time, there is an impulse in the opposite direction, a desire to move into the surrounding world with a positive presentation of the faith in order to create understanding, lessen hostility, and win converts. This development, too, is rooted in the Abrahamic heritage. The call and the promise had made it clear that the purpose of God from the beginning was the blessing, not just of Abraham and his descendants, but through them, of all humankind: " . . . through you all the families of the earth shall be blessed" (Gen. 12:3). Thus many books are written in this period which present to the philosophically trained citizen of the Hellenistic world, as well as to the ordinary citizen who has absorbed the ideas of popular philosophy on the street corner, the tenets of Jewish faith in the thought forms of Greek philosophy.[1]

In both the inward movement toward definition and self-preservation and the outward movement to meet the pagan world, the actual experience of being "strangers and sojourners" in a foreign world becomes an ongoing fact of life that has to be dealt with in the Jewish communities.

THE TRANSLATION OF THE SCRIPTURES INTO GREEK

One result of living in Diaspora was the need to translate the Scriptures into Greek, since that language increasingly came to be the vernacular of the Jews living in Hellenistic cities. While such translations were first made to meet the needs of the Jewish community for worship and study, they inevitably came to serve also as the vehicle by which non-Jews came to know about the Hebrew Scriptures and the story which they contained.

The most important of these translations from Hebrew to Greek, the Septuagint (LXX), was made in Alexandria, Egypt, beginning in the third century B.C.E. It is important to notice how the Hebrew words for "sojourn" and "sojourner" were translated because that gives us some indication of what those Hebrew words meant to the Jews in Alexandria at that time. Furthermore, since the LXX was the Bible of many of the early Christians (e.g., St. Paul) and the version which they often quoted in their writings, the vocabulary of the Septuagint had a considerable influence on the Greek vocabulary of the early Christian writings.

The Hebrew verb *gur*, "to sojourn," and the nouns derived from it, *ger* ("sojourner") and *magor* ("sojourning," "place of sojourning"), were most easily and directly translated by a Greek word group based on the verb *paroikein* ("to inhabit a place as a stranger, live as a stranger"). The related Greek nouns *paroikos* ("stranger, alien, one who lives in a place not his home") and *paroikia* ("the stay or sojourn of one who is not a citizen in a strange place") are very close in meaning to the Hebrew nouns *ger* and *magor*. The translators were clearly aware of the aptness of this Greek word-group for their purpose: they used the Greek verb *paroikein* forty-three times to translate the Hebrew verb *gur*, and in all cases except one, used nouns from this group to translate the Hebrew *magor*. But when they came to translate our noun *ger*, they chose *paroikos* only eleven times (out of a total of ninety-one),[2] and in seventy-seven cases, chose instead the Greek word *proselytos*, ("proselyte, one who has come over, i.e., from paganism to Judaism, convert"). This shift of language shows a change in the way "sojourner" (*ger*) is understood.[3] As we have noted (chap. 5), after the exile the sojourner had been increasingly granted the full rights and duties of the native Israelite and was thus assimilated as a full convert to Judaism. This increasingly religious understanding of the sojourner is parallel to the change in Israel's own self-understanding. Postexilic Judaism, in comparison with preexilic Israel, defines itself increasingly in religious terms and correspondingly less in sociological and national terms.

The word *proselytos* is without parallel in Greek literature outside Jewish and Christian circles.[4] It looks as if it was coined in the Diaspora synagogue, perhaps in Alexandria, to express what "sojourner" had come to mean among those people. The shift of meaning for the word, which had already begun in Palestinian Judaism after the exile, was no doubt accelerated in the Diaspora, especially in Alexandria, where vigorous efforts on the part of the Jews to make a positive presentation of their faith to the local citizens resulted in the conversion of many of them to Judaism.

INDIVIDUALISM

We have already noted an increased awareness of the importance of the individual and an increased emphasis on individual responsibility before and during the exile.[5] Historical factors in the world at large and theological tensions within Judaism itself cause this development to continue. It is seen, for example, in the reflective and questioning literature of Wisdom (Job, Ecclesiastes) and in the piety of the individual worshiper in some of the psalms. This stress on the individual is an important aspect of Judaism during these centuries and must be taken into account in what follows. But it never goes so far as to isolate the individual from the corporate body of which she or he is a member.

DUALISM

Another extremely important factor in this period is the rise of dualism. Here we will deal with only two broad aspects of this development which directly affect Judaism and Christianity.

Apocalypticism

The relation of apocalyptic thought to eschatology is crucial to any discussion of the subject of apocalypticism because the two are so closely related and so often confused. Eschatology is the broader term. It refers to any kind of teaching about the last things, the end time.[6] Apocalypticism is the thought system of an apocalyptic community, arising out of certain kinds of sociological and historical situations. It is built upon a particular kind of eschatology possessing distinct characteristics.

Biblical eschatology in general looks toward the future for God's saving and judging work to be completed in a climactic way. But apocalyptic eschatology is essentially dualistic, and this is one of its chief differences from prophetic eschatology. The eschatology of most of the prophets looks for the coming divine intervention to be carried out within events and through persons in the realm of politics and history. Apocalyptic eschatology, on the other hand, is no longer able to hope for God's final salvation within the stream of history. The tension between the glorious hopes which have been cherished for the future and the bleak realities of the present becomes unbearable. What is expected is deliverance *out of* the present world order *into* a new and transformed order of things, which will be ushered in from outside of history, from the heavenly realm.

> For behold, I create new heavens and a new earth;
> and the former things shall not be remembered
> or come into mind.
>
> (Isa. 65:17)

When the historical and social conditions under which they are living move a group of people to adopt the perspective of apocalyptic eschatology and raise that to an ideology, an apocalyptic community is born.[7] For such a community, this ideology resolves the contradiction between hopes for the future and the harsh realities of the present. The structures and powers of the present evil world are doomed and will simply be reduced to nothingness. The apocalyptic community lives by a vision of the reality of the world to come. The present world, the present age or scheme of things, is passing away. The community's identity is derived from its vision of the coming great deliverance and its expectation of participating in the coming transformation of the universe. "We belong to the age to come. Our citizenship is not of this world."

It is not difficult to see how the sojourner model fits into this apocalyptic view. The member of such an apocalyptic group feels alienated from the present world order and its structures, and confident in the imminent arrival from heaven of the forces which will put an end to the present evil scheme of things and usher in the new cosmic order. Such a person is conscious of being a "stranger and sojourner" in the present age in a sense not previously experienced in connection with these words. Thus the sense of being a sojourner fits the thinking of apocalypticism—with a reversal. In the original sociological context in which the word was born, it was the sojourner who was in some sense temporary or did not belong. In the apocalyptic way of thinking, it is the world around that is temporary, on the way out, or in the last stage of its existence. The apocalyptic sojourners belong to the new order which is destined to replace the present decaying order of things. Their sense of strangeness remains, but their sense of security is intact. They will abide forever when everything now visible will have passed into oblivion.

The dualism of apocalypticism concerns both space and time, but the center of interest lies in the realm of time. Expectations are directed toward the future when God and his host will descend from heaven and bring the powers of this world to an end. And that future is not far away. In the thinking of the apocalyptic community, the end is at hand and the days of the ruling powers of darkness are numbered.

Philosophical Dualism

The second kind of dualism which penetrates Jewish thinking during this period pervades the Hellenistic world. It stresses the duality between this world and the heavenly world, with the latter considered the "true" and superior one. Here the duality operates within categories of space rather than time. The two worlds exist side by side at the same time and throughout time. It is the heavenly, spiritual world, or the world of ideas which is the true and eternal one. The physical, visible world of matter is a shadow or copy of that true world, and may be real and lasting only insofar as it participates in that model heavenly world, which is the realm of mind and spirit, of beauty and truth.

This kind of dualism may have originated in Persian religion. But in the Hellenistic world, where its effect on Judaism first becomes apparent, its influence has come through Platonic philosophy, and particularly a brand of Stoic thought which had worked its way to an accommodation with Platonic dualism.[8] It was this kind of Platonic Stoicism which was popular in Alexandria, Egypt, when a Jewish philosopher named Philo rose to prominence there. It was Philo who gave it clear expression in his teaching and in his many writings. He not only reflected this fusion of Stoic with Platonic thought, but he also attempted to combine this philosophy with Jewish religion. In particular, he used the method of allegory to interpret the Hebrew Scriptures in terms of the categories of his Greek philosophy.[9]

For Philo, the duality between this world and the heavenly world was paralleled by a similar duality between body and soul, between matter and spirit (or mind). Philo, like many of his contemporaries, viewed the body as the tomb of the soul. But the body was considered to be only the temporary residence in which the soul dwells as a stranger or sojourner on earth. The soul's objective is to return to its true home in heaven. Philo wrote a great deal about Abraham as a model for the righteous or wise person, because he saw all wise persons on earth as sojourners, like Abraham, who seek to escape from the domination of the body through meditation, and return to the heavenly realm in mystical flight.

In his treatise on the *Migration of Abraham*, Philo gave an allegorical interpretation of Gen. 12:1–6. Abraham is seen as a type of the human soul (or mind, *nous*) which is called upon to have faith in the promise of God and migrate to the land of virtue. The land which is left behind is the body. The goal of the migration is called the land of virtue, the father's land, the land of the holy word, or the land of wisdom. The soul moves toward its goal by mystical meditation, setting itself free from the dominion of the body. When this has been achieved, the soul has arrived at its true home from which it so long before departed. Thus the departure of the soul from the body at death to return to its heavenly home forever is simply the final stage in an emancipation already achieved.

Philo used the vocabulary of sojourning from the Bible, but it is obvious that the biblical frames of reference (sociological, legal, and religious) in which these words functioned had been left far behind. The otherworldly, flesh-denying dualism of Philo differs from the Bible's positive appreciation of the physical creation, and its assertion of God's approval of the world of matter and God's sovereignty over it.

GLORIFICATION OF HEROES

A fifth factor is the emergent tendency to lift up the great figures of Israel's past, praise them for their achievements, and regard them as models for the present (see chap. 5). The Chronicler glorified David, his supreme hero from the past.[10] But he also spoke of Abraham in warm, if restrained, words of praise (Neh. 9:7–8). The tendency is carried still further in Sirach's praise of famous men (Sirach 44—50), and in Mattathias's death-bed exhortation to his sons to remember the deeds of their ancestors (1 Macc. 2:51–64). Then there is Tobit's instruction to his son Tobias to follow the example of the patriarchs by choosing a wife from among his own people. Noah, Abraham, Isaac, and Jacob are named, but, needless to say, not Esau (Tob. 4:12–13).

One scholar has observed that the use of these figures from the past in the literature of Hellenistic Judaism does not come primarily from biographical motives. It is not merely for the sake of giving them honor and praise. Rather, they have become paradigms of the righteous person, and are used for didactic, polemical, or exhortatory purposes.[11]

This elevation of figures from the past as heroes and models is quite a different thing from the concept of corporate personality (see chap. 1). In that earlier age, we noted that one person could be thought of as embodying the life and destiny of the whole people. There was a sense of psychic unity between the "one" (primary ancestor, or later, king) and the "many" (descendants or subjects). That unity was assumed. It was spontaneous and subconscious. The fact that now, in the Greco-Roman period, the ancestors can be lifted up as heroes and models shows how completely that earlier sense of psychic unity has broken down. Here we have conscious reflection and deliberate metaphorical interpretation. The earlier, subconscious sense of identity with those corporate personalities is gone. Now those "heroes of faith" become models for behavior, to be admired and imitated.

This tendency results in the production of a large number of books during this period which bear the names of the great heroes of the past, particularly the "testaments" and "apocalypses" which bear names that go all the way from Adam to Ezra.[12]

Abraham, in particular, is singled out for considerable attention in this way. The story of his and Sarah's life is greatly elaborated on. Pious imagination supplies countless details which the biblical narrative, with artistic restraint, had refrained from doing. The significance of Abraham's call and journey with the Lord is explored and reflected on for the edification of his descendants and followers.

In this chapter we have attempted to make two things clear: (1) a consideration of the literature and theological development of Judaism in the centuries between Malachi and Matthew is essential for understanding what happens in the period that follows, both in Judaism and in the Christian community; (2) the factors which we have discussed in the Judaism of this period encourage the continued use of the imagery of the sojourner, on the one hand, and the employment of Abraham as an ideal model for life, on the other. Both of these tendencies continue in the Jewish literature of the period which follows. We will now investigate the question of whether the writings of the Christian movement show a similar interest in these themes.

$\equiv 7 \equiv$

SOJOURNER
LANGUAGE IN
CHRISTIAN WRITINGS

TO DISCOVER WHAT the Christian writings (i.e., New Testament) have to say about the sojourner as a designation for the people of God, we first need to review the vocabulary of the sojourner theme.

TERMINOLOGY

Proselytos

We have noted that the Hebrew word *ger* came to mean "convert," and was translated most often in the Greek (LXX) by *proselytos* ("proselyte").

In the New Testament, *proselytos* is used only four times, and it always means a Gentile who has been converted to Judaism. The saying in Matt. 23:15 testifies to the missionary efforts to make such converts. Visitors from Rome who are in Jerusalem for the Feast of Pentecost are described as "Jews and proselytes," that is, those who were born Jews and those who were converts to the faith (Acts 2:10; cf. also 13:43). One of the first seven deacons is such a convert (Acts 6:5).

These proselytes are full converts; they participate fully in the liturgical life of Judaism. They are to be distinguished from the "worshipers of God" or "God-fearers" (Greek: *sebomenoi ton theon = phoboumenoi ton theon*), who attend synagogue and accept monotheism and the ethical teaching of Judaism, but do not obligate themselves to live by the whole Torah, and, if males, are not circumcised (Acts 16:14: Lydia; 18:7: Justis; 13:50; 17:4, 17—*sebomenoi ton theon*; Acts 13:16, 26; 10:2, 22: Cornelius—*phoboumenoi ton theon*). In any case, it is clear that the word *proselytos* in the Christian writings means simply "proselyte" or "convert" to Judaism, and no longer has any connection with the sojourner theme.

A variety of Greek words are available to express the range of ideas originally present in the Hebrew word *ger* and related forms, and in its companion word *tôshab* (see p. 72).

Paroikos

The closest equivalent of *ger* was the Greek word *paroikos* (see p. 79). It is a technical term, from the time of Aristotle onward, for a noncitizen, a resident alien living in a place not his or her home, having no civic rights but enjoying the protection of the natives of that place. *Paroikos* is used in this basic sense in Stephen's sermon (Acts 7:6) to refer to the status of Abraham's descendants as "aliens" in Egypt (cf. Gen. 15:13), and again in the same sermon (Acts 7:29; cf. Exod. 2:22) of Moses' status as an "exile" among the Midianites.

The related noun *paroikia*, meaning "the stay or sojourn of one who is not a citizen in a strange place" (BAGD, 629), is used once in a similar way in Acts 13:17 of "the people . . . during their *stay* in the land of Egypt."

Katoikeo

Katoikeo (same verbal root as *paroikos* but different prepositional prefix) lacks the temporary, alien quality of *paroikos* and its verb form *paroikeo*. The verb *katoikeo* simply means "to live, dwell, settle down, inhabit." The connotation of permanence in this word is highlighted in Acts 7:48 ("the Most High does not *dwell* in houses made with hands . . ."), and Acts 17:24 ("the God who made the world and everything in it, being Lord of heaven and earth, does not *live* in shrines made by humans . . .").[1]

Metoikizo

Metoikizo and its related noun (*metoikesia*), in New Testament usage as well as in the LXX, carry the nuance of "removal" (sometimes forced) to another place of habitation, resettlement, change of abode, as in Acts 7:43: "I will remove you beyond Babylon" (citing Amos

5:27). The noun is used four times in Matt. 1:11, 12, 17, in reference to the deportation to Babylon.

The interest of this word group for our theme is peripheral. It lies in the fact that originally *paroikos* and *metoikos* were synonyms. *Metoikos*, the older term, predominated in Athens. *Paroikos* seems to have predominated in Oriental Greece and adjacent islands.[2]

Xenos

Behind both these terms (*paroikos, metoikos*), sociologically speaking, lies the word *xenos*, which is both an adjective ("strange") and a noun ("stranger"). Both the *paroikoi* and the *metoikoi* were originally *xenoi* ("strangers") before becoming resident aliens in a place. By a process of logical extension, *xenos* also came to mean "host," the one who extends hospitality to strangers (as in Rom. 16:23).

In a number of NT occurrences, *xenos* comes to be closely related to *paroikos* in that it seems to be a broad designation for those who are not native-born citizens of a place. One such instance is Acts 17:21: ". . . the Athenians and foreigners (*xenoi*) who lived there" (cf. 3 John 5).

Finally, *xenos* becomes one term of a word pair which attempts to capture in Greek the meaning of the Hebrew word pair *ger w^etoshab* (see p. 72).

Parepidemos

The other word which frequently appears paired with *xenos* is *parepidemos*. In 1 Pet. 1:1 it occurs alone ("Peter . . . to the *exiles* of the Dispersion . . ."). In 1 Pet. 2:11, it is used with *paroikoi* ("Beloved, I beseech you as aliens and *exiles* . . ."); in Heb. 11:13, with *xenoi* ("They were strangers and *exiles* on the earth"). In both these cases, *parepidemos* stands second in the word pair.

The word *parepidemos* indicates a brief stay in a strange place. In Christian writings, the noun means "stranger, exile, sojourner." In comparison with *paroikos*, the emphasis is on the brevity of the stay. Its use in the New Testament is not an innovation. It was already used in the LXX as the Greek translation for *tôshab* in Gen. 23:4 and Ps. 39:12. Since Gen. 23:4 is surely in the mind of the author of Heb. 11:13, and since Ps. 39:12 is possibly in the background of

1 Pet. 2:11, it is not surprising to find *parepidemos* in these two passages. What is surprising is the fact that the Hebrew word *ger*, the first term of the word pair in each of these texts, is represented by a different Greek word in each (*paroikoi* in 1 Pet. 2:11; *xenoi* in Heb. 11:13).

Allos

Another word group belonging to the semantic field associated with "sojourner" is the group related to the adjective *allos* ("other"). *Allotrios* means "belonging to another, not one's own, strange, foreign." The significant occurrence is in Heb. 11:9, referring to Abraham, who lived in the land of promise "as in a *foreign* land."

It should now be apparent that a number of Greek words and word groups form the semantic field of the term "sojourner" in the Christian Scriptures although none is used with great frequency. Among these, three words stand in an overlapping relationship in the renderings of the Hebrew word-pair *ger w^{e}toshab* ("stranger and sojourner"): the Greek words *paroikos, parepidemos,* and *xenos.*

Greek translators used a variety of combinations of these three words to translate the Hebrew *ger w^{e}toshab.* Likewise, English translators have used a variety of translations for those Greek equivalents of the Hebrew word pair. The following table shows the variety of translations used in the KJV and the RSV for these three Greek words used in pairs.

Heb. 11:13	xenoi kai parepidemoi	KJV: "strangers and exiles" RSV: "strangers and exiles (on the earth)"
1 Pet. 2:11	paroikous kai parepidemous	KJV: "strangers and pilgrims" RSV: "aliens and exiles"
Eph. 2:19	xenoi kai paroikoi	KJV: "strangers and foreigners" RSV: "strangers and sojourners"

But when these same words or related nouns and verbs are used alone, the translations for each are as follows.

1 Pet. 1:17	paroikias	KJV: "(the time of your) sojourning" RSV: "(the time of your) exile"
Heb. 11:9	paroikesen (verb)	KJV: "(he) sojourned" RSV: "(he) sojourned"
1 Pet. 1:1	parepidemois	KJV: "strangers" RSV: "exiles"
Eph. 2:12	xenoi	KJV: "strangers" RSV: "strangers"

Some interesting facts emerge when we study these translations. *Xenoi* is consistently translated "strangers." *Paroikoi* (with related forms) and *parepidemoi* are rendered variously: "strangers," "exiles," "pilgrims," "sojourners," and "aliens." Of these translations, "sojourners" and "aliens" are closest to the basic meaning of the Greek words, as well as the Hebrew words lying behind them in the Hebrew Bible. "Strangers" would be the next choice.

In terms of the movement from strangeness to becoming settled in a place, the progression seems to be: *xenoi, parepidemoi, paroikoi* ("strangers," "temporary residents," "resident aliens"). *Parepidemoi* stands between *xenoi* and *paroikoi*, and can stand in place of either. In English, "sojourner" could stand for either of the last two. "Stranger" is appropriate for the first two, but less so for the third. Once the strangers settled down enough to become resident aliens, their strangeness gradually became less apparent, but it may be a long time before it is completely forgotten. Laws of hospitality toward strangers are apparently universal in the Hellenistic world, but they chiefly have in mind a temporary stay. Different laws come into play for the resident alien who settles in a land which is not his native place.

Of the five translations used in the KJV and RSV for *parepidemoi* and *paroikoi*, "pilgrims" and "exiles" are the least desirable, because each introduces an additional notion which is not necessarily present in the Greek word, and which may or may not be true of the person in question. However, "pilgrims" and "exiles" fit very well into the dualistic frame of thought reflected in the writings of Philo and, to a somewhat lesser extent, into the framework of apocalyptic thinking (see chap. 6). For that reason, they became favorite terms in the vocabulary of the Christian community of the first centuries.

CHRISTIAN USES OF THE VOCABULARY
OF THE SOJOURNER

The specific words for "sojourner" and its synonyms are not used frequently in the New Testament. Our study of this terminology and the path taken by its history has suggested some of the reasons that might account for this infrequency. As in the Hebrew Bible, the uses are few, but striking.

The vocabulary is used in connection with the life of the Christian community in only two places in the Christian Scriptures: Hebrews 11 and 1 Peter 1—2. In Hebrews 11, it is connected explicitly with the source of that verbal image in the Bible, Abraham.

Hebrews

(8) By faith Abraham obeyed when he was called to go out to a place which he was to receive as an inheritance; and he went out, not knowing where he was to go. (9) By faith he *sojourned* in the land of promise, as in a foreign land, living in tents with Isaac and Jacob, heirs with him of the same promise. (10) For he looked forward to the city which has foundations whose builder and maker is God. (11) By faith Sarah herself received power to conceive, even when she was past the age, since she considered him faithful who had promised. (12) Therefore from one man, and him as good as dead, were born descendants as many as the stars of heaven and as the innumerable grains of sand by the seashore. (13) These all died in faith, not having received what was promised, but having seen it and greeted it from afar, and having acknowledged that they were *strangers and exiles* on the earth. (14) For people who speak thus make it clear that they are seeking a homeland. (15) If they had been thinking of that land from which they had gone out, they would have had opportunity to return. (16) But as it is, they desire a better country, that is, a heavenly one. Therefore God is not ashamed to be called their God, for he has prepared for them a better city. (Heb. 11:8–16)

Notice some key features of this passage:

1. Just as Abraham obeyed the call of God and "went out" by faith (v. 8), so he also sojourned in the land of promise by faith (v. 9). His sojourning was by faith, just as his departure had been.

2. The sojourning was not said to be in "the land of Canaan," but in "the land of promise" (v. 9). Does this simply refer to the land

promised to him when he was still in Mesopotamia? Does it not rather mean the land which remains "land of promise" even after he has arrived in it? Obviously the latter meaning is intended, for, according to the phrase that follows, Abraham lives there "as in a foreign land."

3. The temporary nature of his alien residency is emphasized by the fact that he lived "in tents" (v. 9), fragile and transient dwellings, rather than in "the city which has foundations" (v. 10). The land of Canaan is not his true or final home. He looks forward to a city whose builder and maker is God (v. 10).

4. It is also by faith that Sarah is able to conceive and bear the promised offspring (v. 11). Thus Sarah's previously implicit faith is made explicit, and every aspect of the fulfillment of the promises is shown to be by faith.

5. The patriarchs and matriarchs die, not having received the promise (v. 13). But we have noted that in death Abraham and Sarah ceased being sojourners and were buried in a parcel of the promised land purchased from the Hittites (see chap. 1). For the Book of Hebrews, this does not constitute "what was promised."

6. The goal of their journey becomes clarified: they are "strangers and exiles *on the earth*" (vv. 13-16). The author is quoting from Gen. 23:4 ("I am a stranger and sojourner among you"). But the words "among you" are changed to "on the earth," just as they were in Ps. 119:19 (see chap. 5). It is not the land of Canaan in which they are sojourners; it is "the earth." "They are seeking a homeland" (v. 14). The possibility that it might be the land from which they had originally set out is considered and rejected (v. 15). But the possibility that it might be the land in which they are dwelling as sojourners is not even considered. That is not the land they seek. What they desire is a better country—a heavenly one (v. 16).

For the writer of Hebrews, then, the terms of the sojourner imagery have been spiritualized and placed into a framework of dualistic cosmology. It is this earthly life which is the land of sojourning. The promised land is the heavenly one toward which those who have faith are moving with intense longing. Thus the writer has made a new interpretation of the sojourner image in which several shifts from the earlier biblical uses of that image have occurred:

1. The earlier emphasis on time and history has been modified, in the framework of the author's world view, with an imagery that is

primarily spatial. This world is set over against the heavenly world above.

2. In earlier uses, the stress lay on the way in which living as a sojourner affected one's attitude toward all the penultimate realities of life, all of the things which, if regarded as "possessions," might become rivals to the one God in whom alone radical trust may be placed. The center of interest there was on the question of how being a sojourner affects the way one lives one's life before God. In Hebrews the center of interest is in the future hope of the heavenly city, for the sake of which present trials and sufferings can be endured.

3. In the older picture, faith was defined as radical trust in the One who called, and complete obedience to him. Emphasis lay on the relationship of trust in God and in his Word. In Hebrews, faith is as defined in 11:1: "the assurance of things hoped for, the conviction of things not seen." Faith is having confidence in, "betting one's life" on, the invisible, otherworldly (heavenly) realities. Faith here is directed toward the future promised by God, just as it was for Abraham. But the future is now conceived in terms of the two realms, this earthly realm and the heavenly one, rather than as a future within the history of this world order. So faith is what enables one to endure this present age with steadfastness (as did the heroes listed in 11:32–40) in order to enter the heavenly world (cf. also Heb. 6:12, 15 and 12:1–2).[3]

In spite of this shift of meaning, however, faith in Hebrews shares two characteristics that we have noted in the Genesis picture of Abraham's faith. First, faith and obedience are inseparable. Hebrews can say that the wilderness generation failed to enter the Promised Land (or the "sabbath rest," "the Lord's rest," "the heavenly rest") "because of unbelief" (Heb. 3:19) or "because of disobedience" (4:6). The two are equivalent (see the whole passage, 3:7—4:13). Second, faith is so strongly oriented toward the future that it merges with hope, and the two at times become synonymous. Compare "assurance of hope" (6:11) with "assurance of faith" (10:22), and both of these with 11:1 (see also 3:6 and 10:22–23).

First Peter

The passages using sojourner language in 1 Peter have usually been interpreted as operating within a frame of reference similar to that which we have found in the Epistle to the Hebrews.

Peter, an apostle of Jesus Christ, to the *exiles* [*parepidemois*] of the Dispersion in Pontus, Galatia, Cappadocia, Asia and Bithynia. . . . (1 Pet. 1:1)

. . . conduct yourselves with fear throughout the time of your *exile* [*paroikias*]. (1 Pet. 1:17)

Beloved, I beseech you as *aliens and exiles* [*paroikous kai parepidemous*] to abstain from the passions of the flesh that war against your soul. (1 Pet. 2:11)

The time of "exile" is the time of this earthly life. Christians are aliens in this world; they undergo a time of testing and suffering now, but they await their "inheritance which is imperishable, undefiled, and unfading" (1:4), which will be theirs "at the revelation of Jesus Christ" (1:13).

Recent sociological exegesis of 1 Peter has argued that the words *parepidemos*, *paroikia*, and *paroikos* in the passages above must be given the full political, legal, and social meaning which they carried in the Roman Empire of the first century, and therefore must be interpreted literally, not metaphorically. John H. Elliott makes a strong case for seeing the addressees of this epistle as:

. . . a combination of displaced persons who are currently *aliens residing in* [*paroikia, paroikoi*] or *strangers temporarily visiting or passing through* [*parepidemoi*] the four provinces of Asia Minor named in the salutation (1:1). These terms, as their conventional and widespread usage in contemporary secular and religious texts demonstrates, indicate not only the geographical dislocation of the recipients but also the political, legal, social and religious limitations and estrangement which such displacement entails.[4]

Elliott constructs a convincing social profile of these Christians in Asia Minor, making use of extrabiblical evidence that places the *paroikoi* somewhere between full citizens, on the one hand, and complete "strangers" (*xenoi*), on the other.[5] While Elliott may be correct about the social status of these early Christians, it seems likely that the terminology in question would then have a double meaning for them. In view of their situation of political, legal, and economic marginality, powerlessness and vulnerability, and of the suffering which this causes them, the author is stressing both the importance of the Christian community (*oikos*, "household") as a place of belonging and validation in the present, and the coming "revelation of Jesus Christ" (1:13), the

93

time when the chief Shepherd will be manifested (5:4) and his glory revealed (4:13), when the struggles of the present age will come to an end. The very terms which depict their present social situation can also carry metaphorical meaning for them precisely because their hopes are so intensely focused on the coming deliverance. "The end of all things is at hand . . ." (4:7). "Are we exiles and aliens in the society of this world?" they might have said; "truly we are, but that is cause for rejoicing in light of the fact that this world is passing away." The hope offered in 1 Peter is thoroughly eschatological even though the cosmology of that epistle is not the same as that of Hebrews.

In view of the uniqueness of the use of sojourner language in Hebrews and 1 Peter within the Christian Scriptures, we are inclined to ask: Where did this come from? The Hebrew Bible contained nothing quite like this. Only three of the late passages which we looked at might be understood as providing at least some opening in the direction of this kind of interpretation:

"I am a sojourner on the earth." (Ps. 119:19)

"For I am thy passing guest, a sojourner like all my fathers." (Ps. 39:12)

"For we are strangers before thee, and sojourners, as all our fathers were; our days on the earth are like a shadow, and there is no abiding." (1 Chron. 29:15)

Seen in their context, these passages say that it is this transitory life which is the place of sojourning, and not the land of Canaan or even the land of exile. But the Chronicler does not operate within a dualistic framework like that of Hebrews' author. The purpose of his reflection on the transitoriness of life is not to focus attention on the future, heavenly realm, but rather to emphasize the fragility of all human effort, and the fact that all possessions from which offerings are made to God actually come from God himself. Nevertheless, even if the Chronicler does not share Hebrews' cosmology, his language lends itself to the interpretation found in Hebrews, once its cosmology is assumed.

Although the Hebrew Bible itself contains nothing like the interpretation of the sojourner in Hebrews 11 and 1 Peter, we have noted developments within the Judaism of the last two centuries B.C.E. which prepared the way for that kind of interpretation: apocalyptic and philosophical dualism, powerful forces in Palestinian Judaism and in the Diaspora. One or both of these kinds of dualism form the background for Hebrews and 1 Peter.

The language, by itself, might lead us to think that these authors were completely within the circle of the philosophical dualism represented by Philo, but this is not the case. The author of Hebrews has not completely abandoned the perspective of apocalyptic eschatology (Heb. 9:28), and 1 Peter is still completely within that realm of thought. The present suffering is to be endured and present behavior is to be governed by the expectation of the future "day of visitation" (1 Pet. 1:12), "when the Chief Shepherd is manifested" (5:4). In spite of the increasing importance of a dualism of space in Hebrews, the dualism of time persists. Once this background and the abundant literature in which these two forms of dualism are expressed is taken into account, there is nothing in the world view of Hebrews, or that of 1 Peter, which should surprise us.

8

THE SOJOURNER THEME
IN THE CHRISTIAN
SCRIPTURES AND AFTER

WHEN WE TURN to the writings of the early Christians (e.g., the New Testament), we encounter a new dimension to the story of the sojourner. Abraham, the prototype of the sojourner in the Bible, has become an increasingly important hero of the past (see chap. 6). We have seen the prominent place he occupies in Hebrews (11:8–19) in comparison with Moses (vv. 23–28). This prominence of Abraham is true of the New Testament in general. Next to Moses, Abraham receives more attention than any other figure of the Hebrew Scriptures. He is not just mentioned, but is the subject of important discussions (Romans 4; Galatians 3 and 4:21–31; James 2:21–24; see also 1 Clement 10, 17, 31). For the apostle Paul especially, Abraham is clearly the crucial figure in the Scriptures.

Most New Testament references to Abraham do not include the word "sojourner." Hebrews 11 is the striking exception. But with or without the word, it is Abraham as sojourner who stands as a model for early Christian writers. Recall, then, our description of Abraham.

> He heard the call of God, an invitation to abandon the false securities and idolatries of life, and enter a relationship with the One who called him. He responded to that call with radical trust and obedience. From then on, he lived his life on the basis of that word from God which was both promise and command, a word which challenged him to base his life exclusively on faith in God, and to live with his face turned toward the future created by God's promise.

The features of Abraham set forth in this description persist in the Christian Scriptures, as we will now demonstrate.

96

JESUS THE SOJOURNER

Since we find the picture of the sojourner reflected in the life of the early Christian community, we naturally look for evidence of it in connection with Jesus himself. First we will examine his life and then his words, remembering that for Jesus, as for the·earlier Hebrew prophets, life and word, medium and message, are inseparably interwoven.

Jesus' Life

Is Jesus described as a sojourner? Given the nature of Christian belief about Jesus, we would hardly expect to find the term "sojourner" applied to him either in the context of belief that he is the Messiah or in the context of belief in him as Son of God. The word "sojourner" does not influence Messianic imagery in Hebrew Scriptures, nor is it applied to God in the Hebrew Bible. The one time that the Hebrew word *ger* is brought into connection with God at all (Jer. 14:8-9) is to emphasize that God is not like a "stranger," weak and unable to help his people. Nevertheless, we do find that Jesus is pictured in terms which remind us of the sojourner, especially in the context of traditions which speak of him as the Son of man.

> Foxes have holes, and the birds of the air have nests; but the Son of man has no place to lay his head. (Luke 9:58; Matt. 8:20)

The picture which the Gospels paint of Jesus is that of an outsider with respect to the structures of society and the centers of power in his day. A modern sociological study speaks of him as an itinerant charismatic who has given up home, family, possessions, and protection.[1] He lives in the midst of an order and an age which are not his home. He is like a temporary resident living in a place which is not his place of origin, nor is it his final destination. He is *in* the world (in the Johannine sense of the present evil age), but not *of* it, does not originate *from* it, is not grounded in it. He does not draw his identity or power from this world.

This view of Jesus as outsider or resident alien is found in all of the Gospels, but is particularly strong in the Gospel of John. To Nicodemus, Jesus says:

> If I have told you earthly things and you do not believe, how can you believe if I tell you heavenly things? No one has ascended into heaven but he who descended from heaven, the Son of man. (John 3:12–13)[2]

Jesus' sense of identity and his source of power and authority rest in his relationship to his Father in heaven. This becomes increasingly explicit as the Gospel of John evolves:

> I can do nothing on my own authority; as I hear I judge; and my judgment is just, because I seek not my own will but the will of him who sent me. (John 5:30; see also 4:34; 5:19–20, 37; 6:37–38; 11:41–42)

This sense of relationship to the Father fills Jesus' thoughts and is the source of his acts (John 14:10–11). The idea that Jesus is a temporary resident with his destination outside the historical setting in which he lived is connected with this sense of intimate relationship to the Father.

> I came from the Father and have come into the world; again, I am leaving the world and going to the Father. (John 16:28; cf. 14:28–31; 16:5a)

This theme comes to a climax in Jesus' prayer in John 17. Later, in his examination before Pontius Pilate, Jesus identified his true home:

> My kingship is not of this world . . . (John 18:36a),

and his source of power:

> Jesus answered him, "You would have no power over me unless it had been given you from above." (John 19:11a)

After the resurrection, Jesus' first words to Mary Magdalene indicate his intention to return from whence he had come:

> . . . go to my brothers and sisters and say to them, I am ascending to my Father and your Father, to my God and your God. (John 20:17)

As with everything else about Jesus, this sense of being a resident alien with destination outside the present world order is to be shared by his disciples:

> They are not of the world, even as I am not of the world. (John 17:16; cf. vv. 6, 9, 14–16)

Jesus called into being a movement of wandering charismatics—traveling apostles, prophets, and disciples who had taken with total seriousness the call to renounce family and possessions—moving from place to place to heal and proclaim the nearness of the coming Kingdom, and relying on small groups of sympathizers for food and shelter (Matthew 10; Luke 10:1–24).[3] Such groups may form the social context for much of the synoptic tradition, especially its ethical radicalism. Only those who have followed the word and example of Jesus by practicing radical renunciation of home, family, possessions, and rights of protection—who live, in short, on the margin of normal society—can hand on his ethical teachings with total credibility.[4]

This status as outsiders will inevitably produce persecution for them, just as it has for him.

> If the world hates you, know that it has hated me before it hated you. If you were of the world, the world would love its own; but because you are not of the world, but I chose you out of the world, therefore the world hates you. Remember the word that I said to you, "A servant is not greater than his master." If they persecuted me, they will persecute you; if they kept my word, they will keep yours also. (John 15:18–20; cf. Matt. 5:11–12; 10:16–39; Luke 10:10–16)

But this persecution can be endured, because it is a sign of their identity with him, their true belonging to the heavenly world, and because he will return to take them to their heavenly home.

> And when I go and prepare a place for you, I will come again and will take you to myself, that where I am you may be also. (John 14:3)

This sense of the temporary, alien status of the follower of Jesus also permeates the First Epistle of John (see 1 John 2:15, 17, 18a). But it is not limited to the Johannine literature. We find it scattered throughout the Pauline epistles as well.

> . . . the appointed time has grown very short. . . . For the form of this world is passing away. (1 Cor. 7:29–31; see also 2 Cor. 5:1–2, 4a; 1 Thess. 4:16–18; Col. 1:5)

The world view which the apostle Paul here expresses is in harmony with that of other apocalyptic writers (see chap. 6), and locates the young Christian community among the Jewish apocalyptic movements of the first century. There was great variety, of course, among those communities, and the unique qualities of the early Christian movement are well known. But in general, Jesus and his followers share with other apocalyptic movements the following outlook: their true homeland, base of identity, and source of power and expectation lie outside their historical age and world order. They consider them-selves "sojourners" on the earth in their day, resident aliens as in a foreign land. This age is passing away.

Even though Jesus can be described as a sojourner, he never ap-plies that particular word to himself in the received traditions. But in Matt. 25:31–46, he does apply to himself as Son of man another word which belongs to the semantic field of "sojourner" in the New Testa-ment (see chap. 7). At the Great Judgment the nations have been separated, like sheep and goats, on the right hand and the left. After blessing has been pronounced over those on the right hand, they answer the King:

> "Lord, when did we see thee hungry and feed thee, or thirsty and give thee drink? And when did we see thee a *stranger* and welcome thee . . . ?" And the King will answer them, "Truly, I say to you, as you did it to one of the least of these my brothers and sisters, you did it to me." (Matt. 25:37–40)

If Jesus is the King in the parable, as we assume, then he is clearly identifying himself with the stranger (*xenos*). If, on the other hand, the King is the heavenly Father, then Jesus is asserting that just as God identifies himself with the stranger, he, as an obedient child of his Father, would do the same. In any case, final destiny as deter-mined by the judgment is linked to the way one treats those strangers with whom the King identifies himself. This passage is in agreement with the earlier legislation which required full justice and love for the sojourner or stranger in the midst of the community. But in the Torah, the motivating clause for such action was: "for you were sojourners in the land of Egypt. . . . You know the heart of the sojourner." In this parable, the motivating clause is: "As you did it to one of the least of these my brothers and sisters, you did it to me."

Another interpretation is possible, because a difference of opinion exists about the meaning of the words "my brothers and sisters." If it is the Christian community that is meant by these words, then this would mean that among other terms of self-description, the Chris-tian group can be identified by the word "strangers." This would agree with the view of the early Jesus movement as "outsiders," and would be in harmony with those passages in Hebrews 11 and 1 Peter (see chap. 7) which speak of the followers of Jesus as "strangers and aliens" on the earth. Whichever interpretation we accept, Jesus is identifying himself with the strangers.[5]

John's Gospel gives us another line of evidence for the application of sojourner imagery to Jesus. In the Prologue, we read:

> And the Word [logos] became flesh and dwelt among us, full of grace and truth; we have beheld his glory, glory as of the only Son from the Father. (John 1:14)

The word "dwelt" in this verse is more literally translated "tabernacled" or "tented" (Greek eskenosen). The source of this verbal image is the Tent of Meeting in the wilderness, as the second half of the verse makes plain. The glory of the LORD descended upon that Tent of Meeting in the wilderness and filled it (Num. 9:15–16). Moses, emerging from that place of meeting with the Lord, bore a reflection of the glory on his face (Exod. 34:34–35). But the divine Logos, we are told, has pitched his tent among us, and we have looked upon his glory, a glory as of the only Son (monogenes) from the Father.

The connection with the sojourner imagery here is supported by parallels in the writings of Philo and in certain gnostic texts. Philo applies his language of the sojourner or stranger not only to the soul of the individual righteous person, but also to the logos. "The logos itself, like the individual soul, is to be regarded as a stranger."[6]

This idea is developed also in Mandaean and Manichean texts, in which the redeemer god accepts alien status and thus suffering. In this idea, Gnosticism sees a parallel to the individual soul of one who "feels his being in the world is an exile, and who believes that he originally belongs to the divine sphere."[7]

It is not necessary to suppose that the author of the Fourth Gospel knew or was influenced by Philo, much less by these gnostic writers. But it does seem evident that the dualistic frame of reference which permeates the thought world of the first century encourages such parallel use of imagery, even though the Fourth Gospel actually seems much closer to the Hebrew Bible than to Philo.

Jesus' Teaching

In addition to these identifications of Jesus with sojourner imagery, we would like to know what, if anything, he had to say about the subject. We are prepared for the fact that he did not use the actual words that we have examined, aside from the case discussed in Matthew 25. But if we take our description of Abraham the Sojourner and place it beside Jesus' teachings, we see that elements of that picture—the attitude, stance, and spirit of the sojourner—are reflected in Jesus' words.

1. If Jesus himself is pictured as an alien in the world order of his day, the Gospels are full of evidence that he also reached out with love and compassion to all those of his contemporaries who were outsiders and in desperate straits. Under Roman rule, particularly from the Herodian period onward, a large portion of the population of Palestine, and especially Galilee, was desperately poor. Beggars were commonplace. Along with poverty came related ills. The poor were sick, poorly clothed, and hungry most of the time; they were wretched and miserable, lacking life's most basic necessities. The Greek word most commonly used for the poor in the Christian writings (*ptochos*) really means those who are destitute.[8]

Jesus announced the coming Reign of God to the outcasts, the poor and the powerless, the publicans and harlots, and all those whose status in society might be comparable to or even worse than that of a resident alien. It is his special concern to assure such people of God's love for them and of their coming liberation, and to strengthen that assurance by acts of healing, feeding and restoration. He even suggested that these "sinners" were really more fit as subjects for God's coming Kingdom than those in power who despised them, and that these outcasts would enter in while those others would be left outside. It is not hard to see why opposition from those in power would arise against one who talked and acted in such a way, especially when he began to attract a following.

But such a concern for the poor, the helpless, and the weakest members of society was perfectly in line with what Israel had learned about God in its long journey with him. From the day he rescued the helpless slave people in Egypt, the LORD had repeatedly and continually declared himself to be the God who took special care of the widow, the orphan, and the sojourner, watching to see that the rights of the weak and defenseless members of society were established and maintained. That was why he had rescued the Hebrew slaves at the beginning ("I have heard their cry. . . . I have seen their distress . . ."). That was why he sent the prophet Amos and those who came after him, when the poor and the powerless in Israel were being trodden down by the wealthy and powerful members of the covenant community. The biblical God had always been the Partisan of the poor, the Protector of the weak, and the Powerful Deliverer of the powerless. Hence Jesus' attitude and actions toward the outcasts and the despised of his day is simply a reflection and an embodiment of what Israel had always known about its God.

2. The *call* for a complete break from the past, or from the evil world-order, to a life of radical trust and obedience, is frequently heard on Jesus' lips.

> If any one comes to me and does not hate his own father and mother and wife and children and brothers and sisters, yes, and even his own life, he cannot be my disciple. Whoever does not bear his own cross and come after me, cannot be my disciple. . . . Whoever of you does not renounce all that he has cannot be my disciple. (Luke 14:26–27, 33)

> And Jesus said to them, "Follow me and I will make you fishers of human beings." (Mark 1:17; cf. 2:14)

3. The centrality of relationship, both to God and to fellow humans, is everywhere evident in Jesus' teachings.

> Pray, then, like this: Our Father. . . . (Matt. 6:9)

> Jesus answered, "The first [commandment] is, 'Hear, O Israel: The LORD our God, the LORD is one; and you shall love the LORD your God with all your heart, and with all your soul, and with all your mind, and with all your strength.' The second is this, 'You shall love your neighbor as yourself.' There is no other commandment greater than these." (Mark 12:29–31)

> Greater love has no one than this, that one should lay down one's life for one's friends. You are my friends if you do what I command you. (John 15:13–14)

4. Radical trust in God alone is everywhere assumed by Jesus as the norm for his disciples.

> But seek first his kingdom and his righteousness, and all these things shall be yours as well. (Matt. 6:33)

5. The freedom, or voluntary quality of this radical relationship to God is likewise constantly assumed in Jesus' use of the conditional "if."

> If any one would come after me, let him deny himself and take up his cross and follow me. (Matt. 16:24)

> If you would be perfect, go, sell what you possess and give to the poor, and you will have treasure in heaven; and come, follow me. (Matt. 19:21)

> If anyone has ears to hear, let him hear. (Mark 4:23)

> If you love me, you will keep my commandments. (John 14:15; cf. 6:66–67)

6. The centrality of the word in Jesus' ministry is clear.

> He was preaching the word to them. (Mark 2:2; see also 4:14–20)

> The people pressed upon him to hear the word of God. (Luke 5:1)

> My mother and my sisters and brothers are those who hear the word of God and do it. (Luke 8:21)

> Heaven and earth will pass away, but my words will not pass away. (Luke 21:33)

> They have kept thy word. . . . I have given them thy word . . . thy word is truth. (John 17:6, 14, 17)

7. Finally, we see in Jesus' teaching an emphasis on time more than space, and within time, a particular emphasis on the present and future.

> The time is fulfilled, and the kingdom of God is at hand; repent, and believe in the gospel. (Mark 1:15)

> Take heed, watch; for you do not know when the time will come. (Mark 13:33)

When we ask, "To which segment of first-century Judaism does the early Christian movement seem to be most closely related?" the answer is, "to the apocalyptic movements or communities." Apocalyptic eschatology looms large in the words of Jesus and in almost all early Christian writing.[9]

There is, of course, a radically new element in the end time thinking of the early Christians. The long-awaited Day of the Lord has already begun, they proclaimed. The long-expected Kingly Rule of God has arrived. In Jesus' life, death, and resurrection, the end time has overlapped the present age, and the days remaining to the ruling powers of this age are numbered. This belief that the Messiah has arrived to usher in the end (*eschaton*) distinguishes the eschatology of the early Christians from that of the Qumran community.[10]

Nevertheless, the dominant thrust of Christian thinking is still toward the future. Early Christians strain their eyes toward the heavens for the return of their ascended Lord. They know that they live in God's Kingdom now, but they still struggle and suffer under the hand of earthly caesars.

> Beloved, we are God's children now; it does not yet appear what we shall be, but we know that when he appears we shall be like him, for we shall see him as he is. And every one who thus hopes in him purifies himself as he is pure. (1 John 3:2-3)

They groan under the infirmities of the present age, awaiting their full release, knowing that the present evil age is doomed but has not yet passed away. Therefore, they live in hope, which is "a sure and steadfast anchor of the soul" (Heb. 6:19). Christianity is faced toward the future and the Christians survive by hope. Thus the Epistle to the Hebrews exhorts its readers:

> Let us run with perseverance the race that is *set before us,* looking to Jesus the pioneer and perfecter of our faith, who for the joy that was *set before him* endured the cross, despising the shame. . . . (Heb. 12:1, 2, emphasis added)

If, as is frequently said, Christians follow the apostle Paul in living between the "already" of the now present new age and the "not yet" of the end time, that does not mean that they are living in suspension. The "not yet" exerts a powerful pull, and the dominant posture is with face turned toward the future.

As a counterpoint to this emphasis on time, there is a corresponding deemphasis of, or lack of attachment to, holy places. The most notable instance of this is in Jesus' conversation with the woman at Jacob's well, an ancient, venerated spot near Mt. Gerizim, the former site of the Samaritans' Temple (John 4:19-24).

This theme persists in the early church. In a sermonic rehearsal of the history of Israel, the martyr Stephen is on common ground with his hearers until he asserts the priority of the tent in the wilderness, and implies that it was wrong for Solomon to build a house for the Most High who does not dwell in houses made with human hands (Acts 7:44-50). Similarly, the Epistle to the Hebrews regards the

Tabernacle in the wilderness as the proper model for worship, and ignores the Temple of Jerusalem (Hebrews 8 and 9). Additionally, in the New Jerusalem of the Apocalypse, there is no temple, "for its temple is the Lord God the Almighty and the Lamb" (Rev. 21:22). This negative attitude toward the Temple in three strands of Christian writing shows the general lack of attachment to holy places in early Christianity.

To summarize, we have observed that the life of the sojourner is the life of the person of faith. Not only are individual elements in the picture of the sojourner to be found in Jesus' teaching. The total picture of discipleship, as Jesus describes it and calls people to it, also corresponds to the outline of the picture of the sojourner.

The Apostle Paul and the Sojourner

If the sojourner's life is the life of faith, then one expects to hear something on the subject from the apostle for whom faith forms such a central concern. Once again, we are disappointed if we look only for the use of sojourner vocabulary. With the possible exception of Eph. 2:12–19, which many people regard as Pauline, we find no use of the vocabulary of the sojourner in Paul's writings.[11] We do find, however, three key features pertinent to our topic.

1. The general point of view expressed in Heb. 11:13–16 and 1 Peter 2:11 is echoed in the Pauline epistles:

> But our commonwealth [politeuma][12] is in heaven, and from it we await a Savior, the Lord Jesus Christ, who will change our lowly body to be like his glorious body, by the power which enables him even to subject all things to himself. (Phil. 3:20–21)

The Christian's true citizenship, the apostle suggests, is not in any earthly kingdom but in God's kingdom. We may infer, then, that they are only sojourners or resident aliens in those worldly kingdoms in which they now dwell. Paul, however, stays closer to the apocalyptic dualism of time ("now"/"then," "already"/"not yet") than does the book of Hebrews. For Hebrews, the heavenly city toward which we are moving is the focus of expectation. For Paul, the heavenly country is the source from which we expect the Savior, who will transform our lowly bodies to be like his glorious body. The difference is considerable. The apostle Paul is fully at home in the thought world of Jewish apocalyptic eschatology.

2. The locating of the Christian's citizenship in heaven is not the only mark in the Pauline epistles of the alien status of the new community. Recall that the sojourner, from the time of the postexilic Jewish community, was usually not circumcised. "This alien status is confirmed in the NT community. Indeed, it is emulated, since circumcision is no longer demanded."[13]

> Here there cannot be Greek and Jew, circumcised and uncircumcised, barbarian, Scythian, slave person or free, but Christ is all and in all. (Col. 3:11; cf. Gal. 3:28)

3. We must, however, ultimately look at Paul's references to Abraham if we would capture his understanding of the sojourner or person of faith. In Hebrews 11, it is Abraham as a hero of faith who is spoken of as a sojourner. The apostle Paul, without using sojourner language, takes Abraham as his great model for those who have faith and are justified (acquitted, "put right") by God's grace.

In the context of his disputation with the Galatians over the issue of faith versus works of righteousness, Paul writes:

> Thus Abraham "believed God, and it was reckoned to him as righteousness." So you see that it is people of faith who are the children of Abraham. And the scripture, foreseeing that God would justify the Gentiles by faith, preached the Gospel beforehand to Abraham, saying, "In you shall all the nations be blessed." So then, those who are people of faith are blessed with Abraham who had faith. (Gal. 3:6-9; cf. vv. 28-29)

A fuller exposition of what Paul means by the faith of Abraham is set forth in Romans 4. The life of the sojourner who responds to God's call with faith and obedience, leaving behind all idolatries and false securities, trusting entirely in God and his word of promise, corresponds closely to what St. Paul here calls the life of faith. Abraham, the sojourner in the land, is the father of all who have faith. As originating patriarch and as representative person, Abraham is a type of all the people of God who live in a relationship of faith and obedience to the One who calls them out of all foundations for life other than God and his word.

THE EARLY CHURCH AS SOJOURNER
IN THE WORLD

Early Christians apply to their communities two very different terms borrowed from political language: *ekklesia* ("assembly") and *paroikia* ("stay," "sojourn," "place of sojourning"). When the primary reference is to God, the community is *ekklesia* (from the verb "to call out"), an assembly called together by the announcement of the Good News. When the primary reference is to the world and its political structures, the Christian group is called *paroikia*, a community of sojourners who reside temporarily in a country which is not their native land. "For here we have no continuing city, but we seek one to come" (Heb. 13:14).

The Epistle to the Hebrews, in particular, is dominated by the concept of journey within its framework of Hellenistic dualism. If the origin of that concept is Israel's long journey with God, it is fulfilled for Hebrews in the story of Jesus himself, who comes from a foreign place for a temporary stay in this world and then returns to his place of origin. This history shapes the character of the Christian community, its relation to structures of this world, and its piety and liturgy. The conflict that the prophets had with worship that was tied to and dependent upon holy places finds new expression here. The historical uniqueness of Jesus' earthly life is maintained (Heb. 7:27; 9:12, 28), but the true sanctuary is now heaven into which Jesus the High Priest has entered with his own sacrificial blood. Thus Christian worship and piety are loosed from particular places, just as the Christian's loyalty is fixed outside the political structures of this world.

Another word from the experience of Israel borrowed to express this sense of the church's character is Diaspora ("dispersion"). First Peter is addressed "to the elect aliens (*parepidemois*) of the Dispersion in Pontus, Galatia, Cappadocia, Asia and Bithynia" (1 Pet. 1:1). James carries the idea even further, addressing his work "to the twelve tribes in the Diaspora" (James 1:1).[14] It is not impossible that James is addressing his work to the Jews of the Dispersion. But it seems more likely that he has borrowed the terminology of the Diaspora to refer to the Christian communities that are literally dispersed in various places and are regarded as alien communities in the world in which they are living.

After the New Testament period, their writings reveal that Christians continue to think of themselves as an alien colony in the world, as in the *Letter to Diognetus.*

> For Christians cannot be distinguished from the rest of the human race
> by country or language or customs . . . Yet although they live in
> Greek and barbarian cities alike, as each one's lot has been cast, and
> follow the customs of the country in clothing and food and other
> matters of daily living, at the same time they give proof of the remark-
> able and admittedly extraordinary constitution of their commonwealth
> [politeia]. They live in their own countries, but only as aliens [paroikoi].
> They have a share in everything as citizens [politai], and endure every-
> thing as foreigners [xenoi]. Every foreign land is their fatherland, and
> yet for them every fatherland is a foreign land.[15]

A significant development occurs when the word *paroikia* begins
to appear in the plural form. As long as it remained in the singular,
paroikia (originally, "the stay or sojourn in a strange place of one who
is not a citizen") denoted the alien state of the community, the character of the church as an alien body, or the situation of the individual
member as a stranger or sojourner. But according to Eusebius (*Eccle-
siastical History* 5,24.14; 5,18.9), Irenaeus calls Christian churches
paroikiai (pl.), and so does Apollonius. The *Martyrdom of Polycarp*
illustrates the development:

> The Church of God which sojourns at Smyrna, to the Church of God
> sojourning in Philomelium, and to all the congregations [paroikiai] of
> the holy and catholic church [ekklesia] in every place . . .[16]

The word *paroikiai* has now become a technical term parallel to
ekklesia. Previously, *ekklesia* had been used in the singular or the
plural, the one church and the many churches as local manifesta-
tions of the one church. With either of these uses, the total church
or the local church could be called "sojourner" with regard to its
character in the world. But now, in this statement from Polycarp, we
have "the *paroikiai*" of the one "holy and catholic *ekklesia*," so that
ekklesia comes to be used with increasing exclusiveness for the
whole church, whereas *paroikia* becomes a technical term for the
local congregation or parish.

The old sense of the verb *paroikein* is not completely lost (so
Polycarp), when the author greets individual churches in this way:
"the church (*ekklesia*) of God which sojourns (*he paroikousa*) in
Smyrna to the church of God which sojourns in Philomelium." But
as the word *paroikia* has evolved through various languages and

across centuries of history (Latin *paroecia, parochia;* English "parish"), it is questionable whether it has retained any hint of its original meaning to designate the temporary sojourn of aliens in a strange land, or the place in which they sojourn. One cannot help but wonder whether the average Christian parish today thinks of itself as a community of resident aliens whose true citizenship and primary loyalties lie outside the structures of the present age and world-order in which they live.

EPILOGUE

WE HAVE TRAVELED the path of the "sojourner" from Abraham in the second millennium B.C.E. to first-century Judaism into the early Christian movement. While its meaning varied greatly as the context and frame of reference shifted, the basic characteristics of the biblical sojourner seem to remain fairly constant, even though the words used to speak of those elements change.

At the heart of the matter is a call, a word of personal address, calling one out of the world of idols and false securities and away from reliance upon anything other than the God who calls. This call is an invitation to a relationship, personal in nature, which contains both promise and demand. If the call is heard and answered, then the life that unfolds within that relationship will be full and blessed, a life of joy and anticipation, continually moving toward greater fulfillment of the promise. It is a life turned toward the future, ever new, ever unfolding in surprising directions. This is life lived "on the road." The life itself is a journey, and security is found not in attachment to particular places or things along the way, but in relationships—to the God who calls us, and to fellow sojourners.

The picture of the sojourner's life is the biblical picture of the life of faith—life lived on the basis of trust in the God who created us and who loves us. Such a picture is as applicable to our lives today as it ever was. As we have traced the biblical story of the sojourner, some readers may have felt more in tune with one historical expression of it, and some with another. The Christian church, throughout most of its history, seems to have been more at home with the Platonic-Stoic dualism of the Epistle to the Hebrews than with the apocalyptic-eschatological dualism of the early disciples of Jesus which was reflected in the Gospels. For some of us, that situation has changed. Some twentieth-century sojourners feel closer to Abraham or to a first-century apocalyptic understanding of Abraham than to Philo of Alexandria, or even to 1 Peter or Hebrews. However we may lean, it seems clear that the picture of the life of the sojourner has important implications for people of twentieth-century societies. We can only suggest some of the directions in which the sojourner model might lead us.

First, there is our response to the mobility of our age. We are, for the most part, mobile people. But it is not just we who move. Everything in our world seems to be moving also. It is sometimes hard to tell which is moving—the train we are on or the scenery that is rushing past the window.

In such a situation of change and uncertainty, people become anxious about roots, possessions, houses, land—whatever represents security in a world in which everything seems to be in motion. To people like us the Bible says, through the story of the sojourner, that all such attempts to "nail down" security belong to the idolatrous world out of which we are called. Only in personal relationships do we find our security. Our ultimate security is in one relationship alone: with the God who challenges us to live the life of faith. Our quest for roots may be an interesting pastime, but it is not a legitimate concern for the people of God. We are not trees! We are persons, travelers, resident aliens, whose God is not tied down to a particular spot, however holy it might be, but who goes with us on our journey and dwells in our tent. An appropriate prayer for us would be:

> Let me sojourn in thy tent forever!
> Oh to be safe under the shelter of thy wings.
> (Ps. 61:4)

A second implication has to do with the large numbers of people who are literally "resident aliens" in the countries of the world today. It is one thing to be uprooted and moving around in one's own nation; it is quite another to have to flee one's own country and become a refugee in another place, or perhaps in a series of other places, trying to find one that will give a word of welcome and a place to live in relative security and peace. There have always been such people in the world. Today their numbers have reached staggering proportions. Estimates run as high as forty-five million, nearly 10 percent of the world's population.

The first word which the biblical story speaks to us in the face of this situation is one of admonition. From Deuteronomy we hear the reminder: Care for the sojourners in your midst and do not deprive them of their rights, for you know the heart of the sojourner; you were once sojourners yourselves.

The admonition to hospitality and humane treatment of the displaced and the refugee is not enough today. The large numbers of resident aliens strain the capacity of host nations to absorb and care for them. Furthermore, the earth has almost run out of new territory to be explored and settled by fleeing refugees. This problem calls people who are shaped by the biblical message to go beyond hospitality to the resident alien to a concern about the factors which caused them to flee their native lands. On the one hand, persistent efforts must be made to promote freedom and political stability and to eliminate the repression and persecution which cause people to flee for fear of their lives. On the other hand, the economic factors which make life unbearable for large numbers of people and motivate their migration must be addressed in new and imaginative ways. Preventive action is necessary along with alleviation of the suffering of those forced to flee. Such action will more likely be undertaken by people who recognize their own sojourner status on the earth, and who remember that it is only an accident of history that we happen to be the settled inhabitants at this particular moment, and "they" happen to be the resident aliens.

Third, there is the land on which we are allowed to dwell. We are like the ancient Israelite; it is difficult for us to remember that we are not, finally, the owners of the earth on which we sojourn or any portion of it. We engage in transactions and devise legal language to hide from ourselves the fact that our claim to any piece of the earth is transitory and really somewhat ludicrous.

> Lord, let me know my end, and what is the measure of my days;
> let me know how fleeting my life is!
>
> (Ps. 39:4)

Recognizing that we are transients, temporary residents, can transform the way we view possessions, set priorities, and administer our temporary belongings. A recognition of our corporate involvement with others in the care and use of the earth and its limited resources, can transform our social outlook and our concern for generations yet unborn who must travel this road behind us. Such a simple recognition can have far-reaching implications for the way land is developed, for example.

A sojourner kind of ecology of the land, air, water, and total environment of planet earth is desperately needed today. But a warning is in order. Some Christian people have occasionally understood the language of Hebrews and 1 Peter ("strangers and pilgrims on earth") to mean that they have no responsibility for what happens to this world and its structures, since their home is in heaven and they are just passing through this world, getting ready for the "real" life beyond this one. Here a strong emphasis on the biblical affirmation of the goodness of the material universe which God created and on our corporate responsibility for one another in our "global village" is greatly needed. Like the Israelite in the days of the prophets, we need to be reminded that we hold the land—the good earth—in trust, as an inheritance. It is ours to use and enjoy as long as we remember who the real Owner is and that we hold it in trust together with the whole human family, those now living and those yet to be born. A genuine realization of our sojourner status in relation to God and this world would exclude any illusion that the little piece of this world that we "own" is ours to do with as we please.

Fourth, as sojourners we should take a more realistic and healthful attitude toward our own death. As individuals and as societies, we spend enormous amounts of energy and money engaging in denial, devising elaborate methods and systems for hiding from ourselves the reality of our mortality. An acceptance of our status as sojourners on the earth, a recognition of the falsity of our self-made security systems and a placing of our trust in the only true Source of security would free us from many of the anxieties which drive us and exhaust our powers.

Finally, as sojourners we also need to be sensitive to our attitude toward the nations in which we live, the territory they occupy, and the structures of their societies. The sojourner lives within these structures, enjoys their protection, contributes to their functioning and well-being, and to the wholeness of life for all members within them. But the sojourner's loyalty, in the final analysis, is not to any society or political structure. The words "in the final analysis" are important. The sojourner certainly owes loyalty and gives of self, strength, and resources for the upbuilding of the society within which she or he lives. But this is clearly understood to be less than ultimate loyalty. All human governments are subject to God's rule. Just as all individuals tend to be idolaters of one sort or another, so all human societies tend to institutionalize idolatry, and the greater the society, the more powerful the idol. The final allegiance of the so-journer is to the One who calls us away from all false or partial security systems. The sojourner lives with a final element of reserve. The state is not God. Neither is any particular system, hierarchy, or way of life. All human value systems finally stand under God's judgment. All territorial struggles, all impositions of power, all efforts to control and manipulate others, are subject to divine review. The sojourner knows this and keeps it always in mind. Human institutions and the humans who make them up, including the sojourning people themselves, stand under the authority of God alone. So lives the sojourner, the person of faith.

Of course the people of God have not always, either individually or corporately, lived successfully as sojourners, any more than Abraham did. Overall, Jewish people have been more successful than Christians in remembering that their final loyalty lies outside the state or society within which they live. Christians have often become so wedded to the reigning political system that they have forgotten their ultimate loyalty. This may have something to do with the Edict of Constantine and what followed from that. The Jews, partly because of their Diaspora-existence across the centuries, have maintained more of a realization that their final trust and loyalty lie outside and beyond the governments under which they dwell. Perhaps this is one of the reasons that Jews have known endless persecution. Governments tend to be threatened and uneasy about a group of "resident aliens" whose absolute loyalty they cannot command. But this is precisely the role of the biblical people of God, both Jews and Christians, when they are true to the One who calls them to follow the example of Abraham, the sojourner in the land.

With the demise of Christendom in Western secular society, Christians will increasingly join Jews in the experience of being resident aliens in a foreign culture. Rather than lament this development in world history, they should see the hand of God acting in history once more, offering them a new opportunity to recover with clarity and sharp definition the true nature of their faith. They should hear the voice of God speaking to them in this historical moment, calling them to shed the encumbrances accumulated through centuries of accommodation to the cultures of this present world order, and to go out from the land of idolatry, trusting in the One who calls with that word of command and promise. For only in this personal relationship of trust and obedience can the people of God discover their true identity, their real security, and their ultimate destiny.

"Go out," he said, "and I will bless you."

NOTES

Chapter 1
ABRAHAM THE SOJOURNER

COMMENT: In notes that suggest further reading, the following have been cited often, since they are frequently available in professional and institutional libraries: *Interpreter's Dictionary of the Bible* (= IDB. Edited by G. A. Buttrick et al. 4 vols. Nashville and New York: Abingdon Press, 1962) and *Supplementary Volume* (= IDBS. Edited by Keith Crim et al. Nashville and New York: Abingdon Press, 1976); *Harper's Bible Dictionary* (= HBD. Edited by Paul J. Achtemeier et al. San Francisco: Harper & Row, 1985).

Other dictionaries and encyclopedias cited are: *Encyclopedia Judaica* (= EJ. 16 vols. Jerusalem: Keter Publishing House; New York: Macmillan Co., 1971–72); Kittel, Gerhard, and Gerhard Friedrich, eds. *Theological Dictionary of the New Testament* (= TDNT. Translated and edited by Geoffrey W. Bromiley. Grand Rapids: Wm. B. Eerdmans, 1964–76).

1. My view of the relation of Genesis 1—11 to Genesis 12—50 relies on von Rad's *Genesis.*

2. Anderson, *Understanding the Old Testament,* 43 and n. 33.

3. This is the thinking behind a death-bed "testament" like that of Jacob in Genesis 49, in which the later history of the tribes is seen as present, embryonically, in the ancestor for whom each tribe is named. See Anthony J. Saldarini, "Testament," HBD, 1036.

4. The Yahwist author (J) of the great epic of Israelite history written at about this time surely believed and meant for his readers to see that the blessings promised to Abraham in Genesis 12 and elsewhere had been fulfilled, at least in principle, in their own day.

5. For an explanation of the custom, see Speiser, *Genesis,* 119–21.

6. These verses are from the Priestly Document (P), one of the documentary sources of the Pentateuch according to the Documentary Hypothesis, which is here presupposed in its broad outlines. The Yahwist (J) is another (see n. 4 above).

For details, see any standard introduction to the OT or Edward L. Greenstein, "Sources of the Pentateuch," HBD, 983-86; D. N. Freedman, "Pentateuch," IDB 3:711-27; T. E. Fretheim, "Source Criticism, O.T.," IDBS, 838-39.

7. On Mesopotamian religion, see A. L. Oppenheim, "Assyria and Babylonia," IDB 1:297-300.

8. For one exposition of this masterful story, see von Rad, *Genesis*, 232-40.

9. Concerning Abraham's descendants, von Rad writes: "The patriarchs who for the sake of the promise went wandering with Abraham were not buried in 'Hittite' soil—in death they were sojourners no longer" (*OT Theology*, vol. 1, 169).

Chapter 2
FAITH FOR PEOPLE ON THE MOVE

1. See, further, James Muilenburg, "The History of the Religion of Israel," *The Interpreter's Bible*, ed. George A. Buttrick et al. (Nashville: Abingdon Press, 1952), 1:294-97; Anderson, *Understanding the Old Testament*, 41-45.

2. On the transmission of the patriarchal traditions, see Rast, *Tradition History*.

3. Such an opinion was typical of the Wellhausen School of interpretation. See Julius Wellhausen, *Prolegomena to the History of Ancient Israel* (Edinburgh: A. & C. Black, 1885), 318-42.

4. See De Vaux, *Early History*, 186-266.

5. See J. Van Seters, "Patriarchs," IDBS, 645-48. See also Thompson, *Patriarchal Narratives*; Bright, *History*, 95-102; William G. Dever, "The Patriarchal Traditions," in Hayes and Miller, eds., *Israelite and Judaean History*, 70-120.

6. The presentation of the biblical story as a drama was developed fruitfully by Anderson in *The Unfolding Drama of the Bible*.

7. Alt, "The God of the Fathers," in *Essays*, 1-77.

8. On the blessing, see Walter Harrelson, "Blessings and Cursings," IDB 1:446-48; and Terrien, *The Elusive Presence*, 74ff.

9. See Cross, *Canaanite Myth*, 12.

10. Cross, *Canaanite Myth*, 4.

11. The priority of the word is a recurring theme of Terrien's *The Elusive Presence*.

12. According to Westermann, "Promises to the Patriarchs," IDBS, 690, "promise" is the most frequent motif of the patriarchal stories. See also "Patriarch," HBD, 756.

13. See Jürgen Moltmann, *Theology of Hope* (New York: Harper & Row, 1967), 102-12.

14. The familiar picture of the patriarchs as pastoral nomads is called into question by Gottwald, "Were the Early Israelites Pastoral Nomads?" in *Rhetorical Criticism*, 223-55; idem, "Nomadism," IDBS, 629-31; cf. M. Weippert, "Canaan, Conquest and Settlement of," IDBS, 125-30; R. S. Boraas, "Nomads," HBD, 710-11.

15. Greenberg, *The Hab/piru.*

16. De Vaux, *Early History*, 105-12, 209-16; M. C. Astour, "Habiru," IDBS, 382-85.

17. De Vaux, *Early History*, 214.

Chapter 3
MOSES, EXODUS, AND WILDERNESS WANDERING

1. See *The New Oxford Annotated Bible*, note on Exod. 3:14.

2. For a discussion of the interpretations given to the name Yahweh, see B. W. Anderson, "God, Names of," IDB 2:409-11. See also Leo G. Perdue, "Names of God in the Old Testament," in HBD, 685-87; L. I. Rabinowitz, "God, names of," EJ 7:674-86. In recent times, it has been established that YHWH (the tetragrammaton) was most likely vocalized Yahweh. Reverence for the Name led to the substitution of *Adonai* (LORD in the RSV) in postexilic Judaism from at least the third century B.C.E. onward, and eventually to other circumlocutions ("the Name," "the Heavens"). A misunderstanding by Christian translators in the late Middle Ages produced the hybrid form "Jehovah."

3. See "Covenant," HBD, 190-92.

4. Wright, *The Old Testament against Its Environment*, 25-26; and *The Challenge of Israel's Faith*, 65-67. For bibliography on this subject, see Terrien, *The Elusive Presence*, 96 n. 13.

5. On the covenant renewal ceremony, see Anderson, *Understanding the Old Testament*, 379-84, 528-29, 558-59; Weiser, *The Psalms*, 35-52.

6. Heschel, *The Sabbath*, 7.

7. See, further, Muilenburg, *The Way of Israel*, 16-17, 31-33, 44-46, 48-50.

8. On the mediator of word and deed, see Westermann, *A Thousand Years*, 75-76.

9. *Torah*, customarily translated "law," is better translated "instruction" in most cases. The habitual, almost mechanical mistranslation of *torah* as "law" is one of the tragedies in the history of interpretation. See J. A. Sanders, "Torah," IDBS, 909-11; "Torah," HBD, 1083-84; "Torah," EJ 15:1235-46.

10. On the shrines of the wilderness period, see Newman, *People of the Covenant*, 55-71; G. Henton Davies, "Ark of the Covenant," IDB 1:222-26; J. R. Porter, "Ark," HBD, 63-64; Y. M. Grintz, "Ark of the Covenant," EJ 3:459-66; G. H. Davies, "Tabernacle," IDB 4:498-506; A. Rothkoff, "Tabernacle," EJ 15:679-88; J. R. Porter, "Tabernacle," HBD, 1013-14.

11. See Terrien, *The Elusive Presence*, 162-86.

12. See Mircea Eliade, *Cosmos and History: The Myth of the Eternal Return* (New York: Harper & Row, 1954).

13. M. Greenberg, L. Jacobs, and A. Kanof, "Sabbath," EJ 14: cols. 557-72; B. E. Shafer, "Sabbath," IDBS, 760-62; D. A. Glatt and J. H. Tigay, "Sabbath," HBD, 888-89.

14. Heschel, *The Sabbath*, 9.

Chapter 4
LIFE IN THE LAND OF PROMISE

1. Westermann, "Promise to the Patriarchs," IDBS, 690–93.

2. On von Rad's thesis that Deut. 26:5–9 is an ancient credo going back to the time of the tribal league and alternative theories, see his OT Theology, 1:134, 169, 297; J. I. Durham, "Credo, Ancient Israelite," IDBS, 197–99.

3. Ellis, The Yahwist, 28ff.

4. The supposed seminomadic background of the Israelites has recently been vigorously contested. Cf. C. V. Wolf, "Nomadism," IDB 3:558–60; and Norman Gottwald, IDBS, 629–31; see also R. S. Boraas, "Nomads," HBD, 710–11. We must be content with a complex picture of the origins of the tribes that came to constitute Israel. Cf. Gottwald, "Israel, Social and Economic Development of," IDBS, 465–68, and M. Weippert, "Canaan, Conquest and Settlement of," IDBS, 125–30.

5. B. W. Anderson, "Creation," IDB 1:725–32.

6. On the "stranger," see G. Stählin, "Xenos," TDNT 5:1–36.

7. W. Weinfeld, "Covenant, Davidic," IDBS, 188–92.

8. G. E. Mendenhall, "Covenant," IDB 1:714–23; P. A. Riemann, "Covenant, Mosaic," IDBS, 192–97; on both covenants, see J. Unterman, "Covenant," HBD, 190–92.

9. This assumes the commonly held belief that Joshua through 2 Kings was put together by a circle under the influence of Deuteronomy and its theology. See D. N. Freedman, "Deuteronomic History," IDBS, 226–28; K. H. Richards, "Deuteronomist," D. R. Bratcher, "Deuteronomistic Historian," HBD, 219.

10. For further development of this thesis, see Frank VanDevelder, "The Form and History of the Abrahamic Covenant Traditions," (Ph.D. diss., Drew University, 1967).

11. See nn. 7 and 10, and Newman, People of the Covenant.

12. For a refutation of the theory of a "nomadic ideal," see S. Talmon, "Wilderness," IDBS, 946–49; R. S. Boraas, "Nomads," HBD, 710–11.

Chapter 5
SOJOURNERS ABROAD AND AT HOME

1. On the form of the prophetic announcement of judgment or disaster, see Westermann, Prophetic Speech, 169–76, or J. H. Hayes, ed., Old Testament Form Criticism (San Antonio: Trinity University Press, 1974), 159–62.

2. On the work of the Deuteronomistic Historians, see, e.g., Anderson, Understanding the Old Testament, 253–55; D. N. Freedman, "The Deuteronomistic Historian," IDBS, 226–28; D. R. Bratcher, "Deuteronomistic Historian," HBD, 219.

3. See T. M. Mauch, "Sojourner," IDB 4:397–99.

4. On the question of the historical, chronological relationship between Ezra and Nehemiah, see the articles on Ezra-Nehemiah in the IDB and HBD.

5. The Holiness Code (H) is a collection of laws in Leviticus inserted into the Priestly source of the Pentateuch. It is usually dated between 600 and 500 B.C.E., and is closely related to the prophet Ezekiel's work. See, however, J. R. Porter, "Leviticus," IDBS, 543-44.

Chapter 6
THE CENTURIES BETWEEN MALACHI AND MATTHEW

1. E.g., *The Wisdom of Solomon* from the Apocrypha, or *4 Maccabees* and *The Letter of Aristeas* from the Pseudepigrapha. On this literature, see Nickelsburg, *Jewish Literature*. See also "Apocrypha" and "Pseudepigrapha" by D. W. Suter and J. Charlesworth, respectively, HBD; C. T. Fritsch, IDB; and M. E. Stone, IDBS.

2. The eleven uses of *paroikos* occur primarily in contexts in which the word is used of the patriarchs or of Israel itself (Gen. 15:13; 23:4; Exod. 2:22; 18:3; Deut. 14:21; 23:7; 2 Sam. 1:13; 1 Chron. 29:15; Pss. 39:12; 119:19; Jer. 14:8). In addition, the word *toshab* ("temporary resident"), used in close connection with *ger*, as we have seen, is translated as *paroikos* in ten of its thirteen occurrences in the LXX. This shows that the original meaning of the words is not totally forgotten by the LXX translators.

3. See L. I. Rabinowitz, "Proselyte," EJ 13:1182-94; D. L. Lieber, "Strangers and Gentiles," EJ 15:419-21. So much did this use of *proselytos* for Hebrew *ger* dominate the thinking of the LXX translators that they even used it in a few passages in which it refers to the Israelites themselves when they were sojourners (not proselytes!) in Egypt: Exod. 22:21; 23:9; Lev. 19:34; Deut. 10:19; Lev. 25:23.

4. See Mercado, "The Language of Sojourning," to which I am indebted for much of the linguistic information in this section.

5. On the rise of individualism, see Anderson, *Understanding the Old Testament*, 420-21, 439-42.

6. See R. H. Hiers, "Eschatology," HBD, 275-77.

7. On this process, see Paul D. Hanson, "Apocalypticism," IDBS, 28-34.

8. For further study of this Stoic-Platonic thought, see J. N. Sanders, "Word, the," IDB 4:869-70; see also D. M. Smith, "Logos," HBD, 572-73.

9. On Philo, see E. R. Goodenough, "Philo Judeus," IDB 3:796-99; J. M. Bassler, "Philo," HBD, 791.

10. On the Chronicler, see Anderson, *Understanding the Old Testament*, 512-15; P. R. Ackroyd, "Chronicles, I and II," IDBS, 156-58; idem, "Chronicles, the First and Second Books of the," HBD, 163-65.

11. Mercado, "The Language of Sojourning," 72-73.

12. E.g., The Testaments of Moses, of the 12 Patriarchs, of Job, of Abraham, of Isaac; the Apocalypses of Moses, of Abraham, of Baruch, of Ezra, etc.; then 1 Enoch, 2 Enoch, the Martyrdom of Isaiah, the Life of Adam and Eve, and so forth. This literature is readily available in Charlesworth, ed., *The Old Testament Pseudepigrapha*; also H. F. D. Sparks, *The Apocryphal Old Testament* (Oxford: Clarendon Press, 1984). See also Russell, *The Old Testament Pseudepigrapha*, a popular introduction to the patriarchs in this literature.

Chapter 7

SOJOURNER LANGUAGE IN CHRISTIAN WRITINGS

Further information on the words surveyed in this chapter may be found under the appropriate entries in: *A Greek-English Lexicon of the New Testament and Other Early Christian Literature* (=BAGD. Edited by Walter Bauer, William F. Arndt, F. Wilbur Gingrich, and Frederick W. Danker. Chicago: University of Chicago Press, 1979); TDNT (see Notes, chap. 1); *The New International Dictionary of New Testament Theology*. Edited by Colin Brown. 3 vols. Grand Rapids: Zondervan, 1975-78.

1. K. L. and M. A. Schmidt, "Paroikos," TDNT 5:841-53.
2. Mercado, "The Language of Sojourning," 10-11.
3. Ibid., 78-80.
4. Elliott, *A Home for the Homeless*, 48.
5. Ibid., 59-84.

Chapter 8

THE SOJOURNER THEME IN CHRISTIAN SCRIPTURES
AND AFTER

1. Theissen, "Itinerant Radicalism," 85-87.
2. On the centrality of "Son of man" for the Jesus movement, see Theissen, *Sociology*, 24-30.
3. This is Gerd Theissen's thesis in "Itinerant Radicalism," later incorporated into *Sociology*, chap. 2.
4. Theissen, *Sociology*, 10-16.
5. See D. R. Bratcher, "Stranger," HBD, 995; D. M. Pike, "Foreigner," HBD, 318.
6. K. L. and M. A. Schmidt, "Paroikos," TDNT 5:841-53; quote on 849.
7. Ibid., n. 43. For more on this subject in the Epistle to the Hebrews, see ibid., 852 n. 64.
8. See Stegemann, *The Gospel and the Poor*, 13-31.
9. See R. H. Hiers, "Eschatology," HBD, 275-77.
10. On the eschatology of the Qumran community, see Geza Vermes, "Dead Sea Scrolls," IDBS, 210-19, esp. 216.
11. In Eph. 2:12-19 this terminology is applied to the Ephesian Christians in their pre-Christian state. They are now "no longer strangers and sojourners but . . . fellow-citizens with the saints and members of the household of God." Here the application of the term is based on its technical, legal sense, and stands much closer to the sociological meaning which it acquired in the time of the Israelite kingdoms. Christians were formerly like the Canaanites in Israel, *xenoi kai paroikoi*, but now they are like native-born citizens. See K. L. and M. A. Schmidt, "Paroikos, paroikia, paroikeo," TDNT 5:851-52.
12. *Politeuma* often denotes a colony of foreigners, according to BAGD, 686, where the evidence is presented, and M. Dibelius is quoted: "Our home is in heaven, and here on earth we are a colony of heavenly citizens."

13. Schmidt, "Paroikos," TDNT 5:846.

14. K. L. Schmidt, "Diaspora," TDNT 2:98–104, esp. 102–104. See also P. J. Achtemeier, "Diaspora," HBD, 221.

15. *Letter to Diognetus* 5.1.4–5 in *Early Christian Fathers*, ed. Cyril C. Richardson (Philadelphia: Westminster Press), 1:216–17.

16. *The Writings of the Apostolic Fathers*, trans. A. Roberts and J. Donaldson, Ante-Nicene Christian Library 1:79 (Edinburgh: T. & T. Clark, 1873).

SELECT BIBLIOGRAPHY

I. BOOKS FOR THE GENERAL READER

The New Oxford Annotated Bible, RSV. Edited by Herbert G. May and Bruce M. Metzger. New York: Oxford University Press, 1973.

Anderson, Bernhard W. *Understanding the Old Testament.* 4th ed. Englewood Cliffs, N.J.: Prentice-Hall, 1986.

———. *The Unfolding Drama of the Bible.* 3d ed. Philadelphia: Fortress Press, 1988.

Bright, John. *A History of Israel.* 3d ed. Philadelphia: Westminster Press, 1981.

Holt, John. *The Patriarchs of Israel.* Nashville: Vanderbilt University Press, 1964.

Muilenburg, James. *The Way of Israel.* New York: Harper & Row, 1961.

Nickelsburg, George W. E. *Jewish Literature between the Bible and the Mishnah.* Philadelphia: Fortress Press, 1981.

Rad, Gerhard von. *Genesis: A Commentary.* Philadelphia: Westminster Press, 1961.

Rast, Walter E. *Tradition History and the Old Testament.* Philadelphia: Fortress Press, 1972.

Ringgren, Helmer. *Israelite Religion.* Translated by David E. Green. Philadelphia: Fortress Press, 1966.

Russell, D. S. *The Old Testament Pseudepigrapha: Patriarchs and Prophets in Early Judaism.* Philadelphia: Fortress Press, 1987.

Speiser, E. A. *Genesis.* Anchor Bible. Garden City, N.Y.: Doubleday & Co., 1964.

Stegemann, Wolfgang. *The Gospel and the Poor.* Philadelphia: Fortress Press, 1984.

Terrien, Samuel. *The Elusive Presence: Toward a New Biblical Theology.* New York: Harper & Row, 1978.

Weiser, Artur. *The Psalms.* Translated by Herbert Hartwell. Philadelphia: Westminster Press, 1962.

Westermann, Claus. *Isaiah 40—66: A Commentary.* Philadelphia: Westminster Press, 1969.

———. *A Thousand Years and a Day.* Translated by Stanley Rudman. Philadelphia: Muhlenburg Press, 1962.

Wright, George Ernest. *The Challenge of Israel's Faith*. Chicago: University of Chicago Press, 1944.

II. SPECIALIZED STUDIES

Ackroyd, P. R. *Exile and Restoration: A Study of Hebrew Thought of the Sixth Century* B.C. Philadelphia: Westminster Press, 1968.

Alt, Albrecht. *Essays on Old Testament History and Religion*. Translated by R. A. Wilson. Oxford: Basil Blackwell & Mott, 1966.

Anderson, Bernhard W., and Walter Harrelson. *Israel's Prophetic Heritage. Essays in Honor of James Muilenburg*. New York: Harper & Row, 1962.

Charlesworth. James H., ed. *The Old Testament Pseudepigrapha*. 2 vols. New York: Doubleday & Co., 1983–85.

Cross, Frank M. *Canaanite Myth and Hebrew Epic*. Cambridge: Harvard University Press, 1973.

De Vaux, Roland. *Ancient Israel: Its Life and Institutions*. Translated by John McHugh. London: Darton, Longman and Todd, 1961.

—————. *The Early History of Israel*. Translated by David Smith. Philadelphia: Westminster Press, 1978.

Elliott, John H. *A Home for the Homeless: A Sociological Exegesis of 1 Peter, Its Situation and Strategy*. Philadelphia: Fortress Press, 1981.

Ellis, Peter. *The Yahwist: The Bible's First Theologian*. Notre Dame, Ind.: Fides/Claretian, 1968.

Flight, John. "The Nomadic Ideal in the Old Testament." *Journal of Biblical Literature* 42 (1923): 158–226.

Gottwald, Norman K. "Were the Early Israelites Pastoral Nomads?" In *Rhetorical Criticism: Essays in Honor of James Muilenburg*, edited by Jared J. Jackson and Martin Kessler, 223–255. Pittsburgh: Pickwick Press, 1974.

Greenberg, Moshe. *The Hab/piru*. New Haven: American Oriental Society, 1955.

Hayes, John H. and J. Maxwell Miller. *Israelite and Judaean History*. Philadelphia: Westminster Press, 1977.

Heschel, Abraham Joshua. *The Sabbath: Its Meaning for Modern Man*. New York: Farrar, Straus & Giroux, 1951.

Mercado, Luis Fidel. "The Language of Sojourning in the Abraham Midrash in Hebrews 11:8–19: Its Old Testament Basis, Exegetical Traditions and Function in the Epistle to the Hebrews." Ph.D. diss., Harvard University, 1966.

Newman, Murray Lee, Jr. *The People of the Covenant: A Study of Israel from Moses to the Monarchy*. Nashville: Abingdon Press, 1962.

Rad, Gerhard von. *Old Testament Theology*. Translated by D. M. G. Stalker. 2 vols. New York: Harper & Row, 1962–65.

Robinson, H. Wheeler. *Corporate Personality in Ancient Israel*. Philadelphia: Fortress Press, 1964.

Theissen, Gerd. "Itinerant Radicalism: The Tradition of Jesus Sayings from the Perspective of the Sociology of Literature." Translated by Antoinette Wire. *Radical Religion* 2(2–3): 84–93.

———. *Sociology of Early Palestinian Christianity*. Translated by John Bowden. Philadelphia: Fortress Press, 1978.

Thompson, T. L. *The Historicity of the Patriarchal Narratives*. Beiheft zur Zeitschrift für die Alttestamentliche Wissenschaft 133. Berlin and New York: Walter de Gruyter, 1974.

VanDevelder, Frank. "The Form and History of the Abrahamic Covenant Traditions." Ph.D. diss., Drew University, 1967.

Van Seters, J. *Abraham in History and Tradition*. New Haven: Yale University Press, 1975.

Westermann, Claus. *Basic Forms of Prophetic Speech*. Translated by Hugh C. White. Philadelphia: Westminster Press, 1967.

Wright, George Ernest. *The Old Testament against Its Environment*. Studies in Biblical Theology, no. 2. Naperville, Ill.: Alec R. Allenson, 1950.